The Blind Eagle

The Blind Eagle
Stories from the Courtroom

Harriet Ziskin

With Illustrations by Jimi Evins

CONTEMPORARY LITERATURE SERIES

EARLY STAGES PRESS SAN FRANCISCO

Early Stages Press
PO Box 31463
San Francisco CA 94131

Library of Congress Cataloging in Publication Data

Ziskin, Harriet, 1933–
The blind eagle.

(Contemporary literature series)
1. Trials—California. I. Title. II. Series.
KF220.Z57   345.73'02   82-5116
ISBN 0-915786-05-2 347.3052   AACR2
ISBN 0-915786-06-0 (pbk.)

Design: Eric Jungerman

Manufactured in the United States of America
First Edition

In the spring of 1979, there were news reports of an animal sacrifice in Bali. Among the animals sacrificed were mosquitoes, water buffalo, and a rare eagle who had been shot by hunters and blinded in one eye. Although the bird was officially protected by the Indonesian government, priests argued that the sacrifice was necessary because there had been so many disasters in the world. They took the eagle to a sacred spot near a temple and cut its throat.

Contents

Prologue: A Sentencing

The ceiling touches the sky. It collects pale light, casting it down to fill the mahogany chamber. A judge in black flowing robes sits below. He folds his hands like a priest. His silvery skin shines.

The room is a sanctum. The tall black chair is a throne. The form on top of the flag post is a guardian angel.

A lawyer gazes up at the judge. He has fair skin and curly hair which makes him look like a novice. He is beside a dark faceless man who is dressed in white.

The judge speaks. The lawyer nods in rhythm. From my seat, I can't understand what the judge is saying. I don't try. I know he's denouncing the man and it doesn't matter to me which words he chooses. I hear the beat. I hear the tone. I watch the dark man's face form. Faint hollows and swellings turn into a sinister leer.

I know a guard will lead the man away.

Five years ago it would have been different. Five years ago I'd have been in Courtroom B watching light spilling out of fluorescent fixtures hanging beneath a soundproofed ceiling eighteen feet high. I'd have seen an American eagle on top of the flag post. I'd have watched a judge settling into a black swivel chair. But today I conjure up a priest turning a man into a devil because there's too much my normal senses can't explain.

They can't explain why the dark man in white is here beside his lawyer. Oh, I know he's to be sentenced. I know he was convicted of a crime. I know a jury listened to the evidence, and it listened to the law, and if it were five years ago I'd be satisfied with those answers. I'm not now.

Five years ago I began covering the Alameda County superior courthouse in Oakland, California, as a freelance reporter. I covered ordinary proceedings and trials. I'd been taught that the courts were instruments for determining guilt and innocence and for meting out appropriate punishment, but against those rules what I saw happening made no sense.

I told myself the wheels of bureaucracy were to blame for my confusion. They were grinding up the meaning of the law. I'd covered the Oakland public schools and Oakland City Hall, and so I saw the courthouse as just another mill. I expected questions such as guilt and innocence to be buried under stacks of paper and lost in meaningless routine. But I soon realized that this wasn't enough of an answer. I was seeing something more.

I was seeing lawyers and judges joking and laughing as they passed one another in the hallways. I was seeing them competing in contests as they conducted their business in court. Now the courtroom was a gamecourt where everyone was a player, where legal questions didn't matter because everything was a game, where no one cared about guilt or innocence because the goal was to win. But that answer didn't satisfy me either. There was still more.

Then one day I saw a defendant protesting his fate. He struggled like a trapped animal, and the judge and lawyers responded seriously even though the charges against him were absurd. It was a jarring scene—such seriousness against such absurdity. The actors seemed engaged in a bitter game. I left the courthouse that day thinking something quite unconscious was going on.

I recalled the story of an old woman who was burning with fever. She spit on a stone and tossed it into the bushes to cast her fever away. I recalled the story of a rajah who had sinned and was tormented by guilt. He washed himself and poured the tainted bath water over a thief whom he then banished from his realm. I recalled the story of an ancient contest, a deadly game where the loser was sacrificed to the gods. I had the vision of priests declaring the man a sinner, then putting him to death and letting his blood soak the soil.

I could see guards removing his remains as the priests sang thanks to their gods for taking away their troubles, for giving them power.

From that day on, the courtroom never looked the same. The carpeted floor became an altar. Fluorescent lights formed a cross. And today in Courtroom B a priest pronounces a man a devil. A guard waits to lead the devil away.

The Blind Eagle

Part I: The Mill

1

The People v. Willie Monroe

It was all wrong. The woman had come to court expecting compensation for the victory won the week before when the young man,
Willie, her 19-year-old son, came through the trial with a hung jury.
No, she'd known the prosecutor wouldn't dismiss the charges against
Willie as he might have. She'd known he prided himself on being
hard nosed. Still, she told me, she believed the judge would let
Willie out of jail until the case was retried, on his own recognizance,
without having to pay, since she couldn't possibly raise bail. She had
come expecting compensation, but now there was anger between her
son and his lawyer.

The woman was in the front row, up against the rail, and her son
was on the other side, close enough to reach out and touch her, and
the lawyer was standing beside him, bending over, whispering so
both could hear. The son, in the white county jail jumpsuit, had his
eyes lowered.

Suddenly he jerked his head up and said something to the lawyer,
and the lawyer replied, slapping the rail, and the son's face flushed
with anger. I'd thought the reason the son was in court that day was
to settle on a date for a new trial. Perhaps the lawyer was telling him
he had to wait in jail. Perhaps there was more.

The trial had been only the week before, although it seemed longer to me. I'd just begun covering the courts. I'd been wandering around the courthouse, up and down stairs, in and out of courtrooms off dark vestibules. I was hoping to see a trial from beginning to end, but all I found were trials in progress—judges sentencing prisoners, lawyers arguing cases, witnesses halfway through their stories. It wasn't until after lunchtime that I happened upon Willie's trial which was just beginning.

The courtroom looked like courtrooms you see on TV. The jury box was on the right. The clerk's desk was off to the left. There was a lot of dark, varnished paneling, and there was the bar, a wooden railing dividing off the spectators' section from the official part of the room. Out the windows, which must have been ten feet high, I could see the Oakland hills in the distance, small patches of eucalyptus and redwood against brown grass, tiny picture windows sparkling in the sun, facing toward San Francisco across the bay, looking out over the wide stretch of flatlands where children ran out of tumbledown houses to play in gravelly lots.

The prosecutor, a short muscular white man with thinning hair, was making his opening presentation to twelve white jurors, telling them what he thought the evidence was going to prove, and everyone—judge, jurors, Willie and his lawyer—seemed to be listening. Willie was black. So was his lawyer. They were sitting at the end of the lawyers' table furthest from the jury.

When the prosecutor was through, Willie's lawyer stood to say he wouldn't open until later. He was a wiry man with light brown skin, whom I immediately recognized as a local politician. His deep voice filled the courtroom, making me realize how quiet it was, with the judge placidly overseeing the proceedings, the reporter lightly tapping the keys of her steno machine, the clerk idle at his desk, the bailiff at his, and in the audience only Willie's mother and me. Willie's mother was in the front row directly behind her son. She was wearing a gold cross on a chain about her neck that slid in and out of the folds of her blouse marking the pattern of her breathing.

At a cue from the judge, the bailiff hurried out of the courtroom, returning a moment later with a slender white-haired woman who was neatly dressed in a green checked suit and who warmly shook the prosecutor's hand. Standing before the clerk, the woman said her name was Loretta Drummond, and she promised to tell the truth. Then the bailiff helped her into the witness chair.

The prosecutor took his place in front of Mrs. Drummond and began his questions, talking softly yet loud enough for the jury to hear. He asked her if she owned a pet shop in San Leandro, a white suburb adjacent to black East Oakland.

Mrs. Drummond replied that she did.

"Now, Mrs. Drummond, did something happen last July 27th?" the prosecutor asked.

"Yes," Mrs. Drummond replied.

"And can you tell us what it was?"

"Yes." Mrs. Drummond glanced around the courtroom, and then she bent forward closer to the microphone. There were tiny criss-cross lines along her mouth and down her cheeks. "It was in the afternoon," she began.

"Can you say what time in the afternoon?"

"Oh, I'd say one o'clock. Maybe it was one fifteen."

"And what happened at approximately one or one fifteen?"

"Well, I was alone and a young black came . . . a black man came in. He was wearing a cap, and it was pulled down over his ears, down around his face, and he had on a long coat. It came to his ankles. He stood there for a minute or two, and he looked around my shop, and he said, he said, 'Lady, I want your money.' "

"Now, this man who came in. Did he have anything in his hand?"

"Yes, he did. He had a gun. He had a gun in his hand. He pulled it out from under his coat."

"And what did he do then?"

"He said, 'Lady, I don't want to hurt you.' He told me, 'Just don't do anything.' "

"And what did you do?"

Mrs. Drummond shrugged. "I went to the register, and I took out all the money. I took it out and I gave it to him."

"How much money did you give him? How much was in the register?"

"There was twenty-two dollars."

"Twenty-two dollars. What happened next?"

"The man said, 'Lady, I'm sorry, but I need a shot,' and he made me sit in the chair, and don't do anything, and he stood. He just stood for a few minutes. Then he put his gun back under his coat and he left."

I imagined Mrs. Drummond in her store in the tidy shopping

center with brown wood shake roofs, so close to East 14th Street in Oakland where windows were boarded up and paint was peeling. She was inside, straightening the pet dishes on the counter, arranging packages of bird seed on the shelf, eyeing the long-coated black stranger, watching his every move. I noticed Mrs. Drummond's hands shaking as she testified about the gun. They must have shaken that day too. They must have shaken when she sat rigid in the chair, staring at the faceless intruder, letting him see the fear in her eyes, watching him slip silently past glass counters and tanks of fat striped fish and cages of fluttery birds. Perhaps she had fingered the bow at the neck of her blouse as she was doing then on the stand. Perhaps she had counted the passing seconds.

"I heard a car start up outside and I got up."

"And what did you do after you were sure the robber had left?"

"I called the police."

"And what happened next?"

"They came to the shop. I told them what happened. They asked me a lot of questions, and I answered them all. I got a good look at him."

"Now, did an officer stop by your shop the following day and ask you to look at some photographs?"

"Yes, he did."

"And were you able to make an identification from one of the pictures?"

"Yes, I was."

"What made you pick out that particular picture?"

"Because it resembled the young man."

"Were you sure it was the robber, Mrs. Drummond?"

"I was sure." Mrs. Drummond was nodding her head. She was sitting on the edge of the chair, which made her look taller. Her hands weren't shaking any more. She said she went downtown a few days afterwards and picked the robber out of a lineup. "He was number two. I knew him immediately. I only glanced at the other four men."

"Mrs. Drummond, do you see that man in court today?" The prosecutor stepped back, out of the jury's line of vision.

"Yes, I do," Mrs. Drummond replied. The jurors all turned their heads when she pointed at Willie.

"Was the robber wearing gloves?" the prosecutor asked. He was at an angle now, facing Mrs. Drummond and the jury, acting as a bridge.

"No," Mrs. Drummond said. "His hands were bare."

"What kind of gun was it?" the prosecutor asked.

"I think it was a rifle. I really don't know very much about guns."

"Was the robber wearing a cap like this?" The prosecutor fished a navy blue knit cap out of a large paper bag on the clerk's desk, and then he stepped back to his place in front of the witness, dangling the cap in the air.

"Yes, the cap was like that," Mrs. Drummond replied.

"Was the gun similar to this one?" The prosecutor picked up a rifle off of the clerk's desk and held it in both hands over his head.

"Yes, it was similar."

The back-and-forth between the witness and the prosecutor took on such a compelling rhythm that I felt cut off from everything else inside and outside the courtroom—even from my own thoughts. It was as though the prosecutor were working some kind of magic. After he ended his questions and sat down, the defender stood and began cross examination without breaking the spell.

"Now, Mrs. Drummond, what time was it that you were robbed?" the defender asked, speaking more kindly than I thought he would have had Mrs. Drummond been twenty years younger.

"One twenty, around then," Mrs. Drummond replied.

"So there was sunlight in the store?"

"Yes. There were fluorescent lights on too."

"Where was the sunlight coming from in relation to the robber?"

"From the back of him."

"Could you see his face?"

"Yes."

"How old was the robber?"

"Nineteen, twenty."

"And was his face narrow or wide?"

Mrs. Drummond glanced at Willie and then at the defender. "It was narrower than most," she said.

"And his eyes?"

Again Mrs. Drummond looked at Willie and then back at the defender. "His eyes were large."

"You didn't tell the police that, did you?"

"Yes, I said that to the officer."

"Did the robber have hair on his face?"

"Yes, some." There was another stolen glance in Willie's direction. She seemed determined to identify him as the robber. "There was hair on his chin, but it didn't look like it had been growing for very long," she said.

The defender turned around and picked up a sheet of paper from the lawyers' table. Facing Mrs. Drummond again, he asked, "Why didn't you tell the police that he had facial hair?" He was pointing to the paper, which I assumed was a police report.

"I did," Mrs. Drummond responded evenly.

"Why didn't you tell the police the robber wore a moustache?" the defender persisted, now facing the witness squarely, his voice a good deal sterner than it had been before.

"I did."

"Isn't it true your identification wasn't positive?"

"No." Mrs. Drummond was insistent.

"Isn't it true there was a glare from the sun shining on the large display window?"

"No." Mrs. Drummond said she was sure that wasn't true.

"The sun was coming from the back of the robber. Wasn't it in your eyes?"

"No." Mrs. Drummond insisted she saw the robber clearly.

"Didn't you pick Mr. Monroe out of the lineup because you remembered his face from the photograph the officer showed you?"

"No." Mrs. Drummond said she was sure that wasn't true either, and the more the defender tried to cast doubt on her testimony, the surer she became.

"Was there another black man who came into the shop before the robbery?" Willie's lawyer asked.

"Yes. There was a nice young man who came in the shop, it must have been an hour before. He asked me if I had any puppies."

"What was *that* man wearing?"

"He was wearing a white T-shirt."

"Did he look at the fish?"

"Yes. He stayed a while looking at the fish."

"And the snakes?"

"No, he didn't look at the snakes."

"What did he look like?"

"He was just a nice clean-cut young man."

"Was it the defendant?"

"No."

"Are you certain, Mrs. Drummond?"

"Yes. His hair was cut short." Mrs. Drummond's eyes shifted momentarily to Willie. "Shorter than Mr. Monroe's."

Mrs. Drummond tucked a stray wisp into the fine mesh of her bouffant hairdo and stared at the jury. She didn't seem to be surprised that the defender knew a second black man had been in her store. She seemed as unruffled as she had earlier when she contradicted the police report. Perhaps she felt safe only so long as she remained convinced that Willie was guilty and would go to jail. She certainly seemed to need him to be the robber.

"I've been to court so many times since they took Willie. I pray a lot," Mrs. Monroe told me as we waited in the marble hallway for the elevator which was forever in coming. She was a small woman who wore her short hair in a pageboy. She told me she went to church every day. She held out a Bible.

There was an uneasy pause as we both fumbled for something to say. Mrs. Monroe broke the silence. "Willie's a quiet boy," she almost whispered. "He doesn't say much, but he likes to tease." She smiled shyly. Then, seeing my smile, she laughed. "He'll start wrassling with his baby sister, and I'll tell him to stop, and he'll come over and pick me way up in the air." She continued on with stories about her son and I realized it was the first time since I'd entered the courtroom that Willie had been presented to me as a person.

Mrs. Monroe grasped her gold cross and ran it up and down along her cheek. She looked around the hallway, at the locked doors, at the bare marble walls. "You know, Willie told me he wanted a puppy," she murmured. "He always liked snakes and fish. He was always bringing those things home, and I'd get all upset and tell him to get them out of the house." She was looking at me again, and her eyes were sparkling.

Then she was serious. I was startled by the sharpness of her voice. "That boy in the shop? The one who was there an hour before the robbery ever took place?"

"It was Willie, wasn't it?" I asked.

Mrs. Monroe nodded. "Mrs. Drummond got the two of them confused," she said. "She thinks all black boys look alike."

The trial resumed the next morning at ten o'clock sharp. Willie was beside his lawyer, looking freshly scrubbed, wearing an orange and beige knit shirt. A policeman was on the stand confirming that Mrs. Drummond *had* identified Willie from a mug shot. On cross examination the officer admitted that Mrs. Drummond asked to look at the photos outside her shop because she couldn't see well enough by the light inside. He said her identification hadn't been positive. She hadn't been sure because the man in the photo had a moustache.

The officer stepped down, and an insurance salesman, a balding man with a round face, took the stand. He said he owned a shop near Mrs. Drummond's and on the day of the robbery he saw a young black man hanging around the parking lot behind the store. "I went to see if anything was wrong," the salesman told the prosecutor. "The man said he was having trouble with his car. There was another man in the car with him."

"What time was that?" the prosecutor asked.

"I'm not sure, sir. It was sometime after twelve fifteen. I know because I'd closed up for lunch."

"And what happened after the man told you he was having car trouble?"

"They finally drove off."

"Can you identify who was driving the car?"

"No, not really. He looked something like the defendant there, sir, but I'm not sure."

"Can you remember what the driver was wearing?"

"Yes, I can. He was wearing dark glasses. Dark glasses and gloves."

The salesman didn't say anything definite. He said he couldn't be sure. But dark glasses and gloves, hanging around, trouble starting the car. That sounded suspicious. Two of the jurors shot glances at Willie.

The salesman stepped down, and Margaret Daniels, a plump middle aged woman with dark hair and olive skin, came hurrying down the aisle, leaving the bailiff behind, taking the stand, adjusting the microphone herself.

The prosecutor asked Mrs. Daniels where she lived.

"East Oakland," she said.

Had something happened to her on July 28th, the day after the pet store robbery? he asked.

"Yes," she said. "It was in the morning, about ten thirty. I was back from Lucky's. I had a car full of groceries. I was carrying a bag up the stairs to my house, and I glanced at a car parked there down 36th Avenue. I saw a man was in the car, he was in the front seat, he looked black, but I guess he was Mexican."

The prosecutor had Mrs. Daniels mark the location of the car on a large diagram he had tacked to an easel. He had her use a blue felt-tipped pen. Then he asked, "Was this man alone in the car?"

"Yes, he was alone, but when I came back out for more groceries he wasn't. There was a second man in the car . . . him." Jurors' eyes followed as Mrs. Daniels jerked her head toward Willie.

The prosecutor asked Mrs. Daniels what the two men were doing.

"They weren't doing anything," she said. She said she went and got another bag of groceries, and they were still there, just sitting, the two of them.

"And what happened then?"

"Then finally they left where they were parked on 36th Avenue, and they went left at the post office over there on Case, and then they pulled into the lot at the back of the liquor store, off Case."

"Now, did you do anything at that point?"

"No, I just watched them for a few minutes, and then I decided this is too much, and I drove my car and turned down Case, and I parked right behind them. I ran across the street and knocked on my friend's door, but nobody was home, so I ran back to the car."

"And did either of the men get out of the car?"

"Yes. *He* did." Jurors' heads turned again as she pointed at Willie who was slouched in his chair.

"And then what happened, Mrs. Daniels?"

"He raised the hood, and he stood there looking under the hood. I drove back onto 36th, and I saw a policeman coming out of the liquor store, and I stopped and asked him to check out the car."

"Why did you ask him to do that?"

"Because he looked suspicious."

"Object! Irrelevant!" Willie's lawyer boomed out. He was stand-

ing. "I object to this whole line of questioning. This has nothing to
do with the charge against the defendant. It can only be prejudicing
the jury!"

The judge gave the prosecutor a questioning look.

"I plan to tie it in, your honor."

"We'll let it stand for now," said the judge. He was a man with
fine features and watery blue eyes who sounded so mechanical I
realized the defender's loud objection was the first open display of
emotion at the trial. The judge had been unobtrusive, the prosecutor
controlled. With the exception of an old man in silver rimmed glasses
who dozed through most of the testimony, the jurors had remained
frozen. Yet underneath the restraint I sensed a tension. And there
was Willie staring down at his lap and shifting about in his chair.

During cross examination the defender got Daniels to say she
hadn't seen Willie or his friend going into the liquor store or doing
anything illegal. Then he had her repeat parts of her story, and he
had her make more marks on the diagram, showing where Willie's
car was when she first saw it, and where it was when he raised the
hood, and where she was and the route she took, but he wasn't able
to get her to back down on a single point. Far from dispelling the
suspicion she'd aroused, the repetition and having her put everything down in black and white made her testimony seem authentic.

Officer Damon, a slight dark man in a blue uniform who looked
about Willie's age, testified after Mrs. Daniels. He was the policeman who had been in the liquor store, and he said that when Mrs.
Daniels told him about her suspicions, he immediately got into his
patrol car and drove around the corner to the rear of the liquor store
where he saw "a male Negro, late teens, early twenties," across the
street, closing the hood of his car.

"Do you see that man today in the courtroom?"

"Yes," the officer replied, and for a third time all eyes were on
Willie Monroe.

Officer Damon said Willie got into the car. "We looked at each
other for a few seconds. The defendant got into the car, and I made a
U-turn to go talk to him." Officer Damon said the car took off and
he pursued it.

"Was he speeding?" the prosecutor asked.

"I don't know if he was speeding or not, but I was under the
impression he was trying to elude me," Officer Damon replied. He

said he called downtown for backup support, then he put on his flashing red light and siren and Willie pulled over to the curb. "He looked upset."

"Did you ask him for his ID?"

"Yes. He didn't have any. I had him step back to my vehicle and, after my cover came, I asked him for his name and date of birth."

Officer Mingo was Officer Damon's cover. He testified too, following Damon so quickly it was as if one person were telling the story.

"When I got there Officer Damon was questioning the suspect," Mingo told the prosecutor. He said he began searching Willie's car. He reached through the open window to pull the keys out of the ignition, and he went around to the back and opened the trunk where he found rifle shells loose on the floor. He looked down at the license plate, he walked around to look at the front license plate too, and he found the numbers were altered with black tape. As the officer testified I studied Willie, craning my neck to see his face. I realized that nothing had happened in the courtroom to connect me to him as a person. There he was in his orange and beige shirt sitting like a lump of clay, waiting to take on whatever contours the witnesses and lawyers gave him. If I'd been a juror, I'd have found it hard *not* to imagine him in a long dark coat, slipping silently out of Mrs. Drummond's store.

Officer Mingo said he opened the driver's door, and he bent over to look inside the car. He found a blue knit cap and gloves and a woman's gold watch and an empty paper bag and a tape deck under the front seat and sunglasses on the dash and a roll of black tape which matched the tape on the license plate. He closed the door and told the suspect he was under arrest.

During the noontime break Mrs. Monroe and I took our sandwiches to the edge of the lake behind the courthouse where we basked in the sun and the stillness and watched ducks slip across the water leaving behind them a design of ever widening circles. "They're turning such small things into big things," she said sadly. "You know, Willie asked to have a lie detector test, but it costs too much." She stared ahead, seeming to have forgotten I was there.

All at once she pointed at a man walking down the path, maybe twenty feet away. "Do you see that man over there?" She tugged my arm, not waiting for a reply. "Now, doesn't he look just like the judge, gray hair, dark suit and all? The other day I walked up to him and asked him when he was going to let Willie come home, and he said, 'What are you talking about?' He looked at me like I was crazy. I said, 'Aren't you the judge?' 'No,' he said, 'I'm not him.' " The words were lost in her laughter.

"And you were so positive," I said.

Mrs. Monroe nodded.

"You know, this morning's testimony left me completely confused," I told Mrs. Monroe. "I don't understand why the judge allowed it." I'd had time to think about what the witnesses had said. I realized I was angry. In a trial the burden of proof was supposed to be on the prosecution, or so I'd been taught, but here was Willie buried under a heap of innuendoes. Willie acting suspiciously in the parking lot. Willie acting suspiciously behind the liquor store. Willie wearing dark glasses and gloves. Willie under arrest (the policeman never did explain why). Willie was going to be hard to defend. I wanted to tell Mrs. Monroe, but I was afraid I might upset her.

"I think the defender was right," I told her. "The prosecutor was trying to prejudice the jury."

"That prosecutor wants to win. He'll do anything he can to put Willie in jail." Mrs. Monroe shrugged. "He's trying to make Willie out to be a suspicious character."

"Yes," I agreed. "It doesn't seem to matter whether or not he has proof. He's making everything fuzzy." Like a tree in the fog, I thought. You can't see the bark or the leaves, and you imagine it's twice as big as it really is.

We returned from lunch early to find Willie already down from the courthouse jail on the tenth floor. Since no one else was in the courtroom, the bailiff let Willie sit near the bar where he could talk to his mother. He was neat and scrubbed, looking fresh in gray pants and a gray and white shirt, laughing, teasing, like his mother had said. It was almost time for him to testify in his own behalf, but if he was nervous about it he wasn't letting his mother know.

The clerk returned from lunch, followed soon after by the court reporter who stopped at the bailiff's desk to show him the afternoon paper. Pretty soon the two were talking excitedly, and the excitement grew when the defender came in and everybody crowded around him and began shaking his hand. I later learned the afternoon papers announced his appointment to an office high up in the state bureaucracy.

Willie was back at the lawyers' table, the laughter drained from his face. I noticed a scar on his forehead angling down over his left eye like the edge of a thick knife. When he finally took the stand, he told his story quickly, leaning forward toward the microphone, his arms resting along the arms of the chair.

Yes, Willie said, he *had* been in the pet store, around noontime, about an hour before the robbery. He drove there with his friend, David Sanchez, in his mother's '63 Plymouth. He parked and went into the liquor store on the corner for a pack of gum, and then he went inside the pet shop looking for a puppy. When Mrs. Drummond told him she didn't have any puppies, Willie said he stayed for a few minutes to look at the fish and the snakes. He said he could remember tapping on the snake tank to make the snakes move. He and David went home to East Oakland for lunch. They listened to music for a while before driving off again to keep Willie's two o'clock court appointment in Berkeley.

"Were you on time for your appointment?" the defender asked.

"Yes," Willie replied.

"What were you wearing when you went into the pet store?" The defender had changed the subject. I wondered why he'd brought up Willie's court appointment if he wasn't going to have Willie explain what it was for.

"I was wearing a blue shirt and brown bell bottoms," Willie replied.

"Were you wearing a hat?"

"No. I *never* wear hats unless my hair's not done up."

"How long have you been in jail?"

"For three months. Since they arrested me."

"Are you a dope addict?"

"No." Willie shook his head.

"Have you had any withdrawal symptoms?"

"No."

"Mr. Monroe. Can you tell the jury why you were outside the liquor store on 36th Avenue last July 28th?"

Willie explained that he had stopped in the store to buy a bottle of orange juice, and he was drinking the juice in his car. He said he was

with his friend David again, and the two of them were just sitting
and talking. Willie said he didn't realize the policeman was following
him until he heard the siren. He pulled over right away.

"Were you trying to run away?"

"No." Willie shook his head.

"Were you trying to change the numbers on your license plate?"

"No." Willie told the defender the sunglasses and the gloves the
police found in his car were his, but the cap was David's. "I don't
own a cap like that," Willie said.

"How were you wearing your hair last July?"

"A curly natural."

"Would you explain to the jury what that means?"

Willie described how his hair looked, shorter than it was now, and
how black people fix their hair. One of the older jurors looked down
in her lap while Willie gave his explanation.

As the defender stepped back to his seat I thought about what
Willie had said. The robbery was at one fifteen, which gave Willie
about fifteen minutes more than he needed to make a two o'clock
appointment in the Berkeley municipal courthouse. Willie wasn't
going to have an alibi unless there was someone else to verify that he
had stopped off at home long enough for lunch. Meanwhile, I wondered why he'd had to appear in court in Berkeley.

"How long have you known David Sanchez?" the prosecutor
asked. It was his turn now for cross examination. He pushed back
his chair and stood behind the lawyers' table, peering down at some
notes.

"For six months," Willie replied.

"The police found bullets in the back of your car." The prosecutor's head was up and he was staring at Willie.

"Yes. They're for huntin'." Willie pressed up against the back of
the chair.

"You own a gun?"

"Yes."

"Similar to this one?" The prosecutor stepped over to the clerk's
desk to pick up the gun that Mrs. Drummond had said looked like
the one the robber used.

"I guess."

"When did you last see David Sanchez?"

"I seen him in jail." Willie was mumbling.

"Where? Speak up!" The prosecutor cupped his hand to his ear as he moved over by the railing in front of the jury box.

"I seen him in jail." Still barely audible.

"Do you know David Sanchez is waiting to go to trial for robbery?" The prosecutor quickly glanced down as the defender jumped up and, in a booming voice, demanded a mistrial, and the judge calmly told the jurors the prosecutor's question was improper. They should put it out of their minds.

Propping himself up on the edge of the lawyers' table closest to the jury box, the prosecutor had Willie retell his story. Was Willie the man the insurance salesman had seen in the parking lot, he asked. Yes, Willie replied. Why was Willie in the parking lot for so long, the prosecutor wanted to know. His car was stalled, Willie replied. Was he wearing sunglasses? Yes, he was. And gloves? Yes. Was the tape deck Officer Mingo found under the seat of the car his? Yes, the tape deck was his. And the knit cap? No, he didn't own a knit cap. ("Notice how he's not asking about the lady's gold watch," Mrs. Monroe whispered in my ear. "He was going to get the jury to wonder what's a poor black boy doing with a lady's gold watch, but I told him the watch was mine and Willie was taking it for me to get it fixed. Notice how he's not saying anything about that.")

The prosecutor moved closer to Willie. He asked him why Officer Damon found him in back of the liquor store looking under the hood of his car.

"I was fixin' the wire to the tail light."

"Did you check after you fixed it to see if the tail light was working?"

"No."

"No?" Grinning, the prosecutor glanced at the jury. "Why was it you had all those bullets in the trunk of your car?" he asked Willie.

"To go huntin'."

"Where?"

"Out to Martinez."

"Huntin' in Martinez?" The prosecutor's eyes bulged. "Do you go huntin' there often?" he chuckled and took a few steps back. The juror in the back row, the woman with short gray hair, looked at her hands in her lap and smiled.

"I never been huntin' before." Willie's knee was jogging up and down.

"When was the last time you used the gun?"

"On the Fourth of July. I shot it into the ground."

"You shot it into the ground! Don't you know that's a crime?"

Willie was clutching the arms of the chair. Two damp circles darkened the underarms of his fresh shirt, and drops of perspiration glistened along the edges of his scar.

On redirect examination the defender asked Willie if he'd worn a moustache the summer before (Willie said yes), and he had Willie explain that when he'd gone to court in Berkeley, the charges against him had been dismissed. The defender sat down. The prosecutor declined further cross examination. The judge excused Willie from the stand, and then the defender stood up again to announce that he had no more witnesses, catching me completely by surprise. I'd known Willie was going to be hard to defend, but I wasn't prepared for the defender to leave him seeming so guilty.

Out by the elevator I introduced myself to the defender. It was crowded and noisy. It seemed every courtroom had recessed at the same time. A crowd of people poured out of the elevator, a jury panel summoned to the courtroom across the hall. The defender agreed to answer my questions. As I was opening my notebook and fishing a pen out of my purse, a man with a briefcase approached him, congratulating him on his important new job. They talked for a moment. Then I began the interview.

I asked the defender why he had decided not to put other witnesses on the stand. Weren't there people who could have vouched for Willie's character? I told him Mrs. Monroe had told me Willie was back in school and he had a job at the cannery.

"No. You're opening up a can of worms. That wasn't last summer. He wasn't employed last summer. If I'd opened that up, then the prosecutor would have been able to bring out that on the day of the robbery Willie wasn't enrolled in any school, and he was very much unemployed. He needed money."

"What about the gun?" I asked. "Where did it come from?" The defender had objected to the prosecutor displaying the gun, saying there was no evidence linking it to the robbery, but the judge had overruled the objection.

"The police found it when they searched the car," he replied.

"Why didn't the prosecutor have one of the witnesses say that?"

"Because the search was illegal. The police arrested Willie for illegal possession of a gun. But the search was illegal, and a public defender got the evidence suppressed and the charge dismissed. He didn't get the other evidence suppressed, the bullets and the hat, because it didn't seem important at the time."

"But even if the jury knew the gun was Willie's, there's still nothing linking it to the robbery."

"That's right."

A man brushed past me. I reached out to catch my purse strap which began sliding off my shoulder. "Did you consider calling in an expert witness to explain to the jury how unreliable eye witness identifications usually are?" I asked. I'd read somewhere about a study which proved that.

"Experts cost a hundred dollars a day," he said. "This is a poor man's defense. Poor people have to rely on the fairness of the jury."

"Why is the jury all white?" I asked the defender.

"Why? There were five blacks on the original panel. Two disqualified themselves, said they couldn't be fair. The prosecutor excused the rest. He told me afterwards he didn't think blacks could be objective when the defendant was black."

"Do you think Willie is guilty?" I asked.

"Not of *this* charge." The defender turned away to say hello to another man with a briefcase.

"An old woman afraid for her life. Does she remember the robber? There's no way she'd ever forget." The prosecutor was summarizing his case for the jury. He was pacing back and forth in front of the jury box, taking short bouncy steps. "What's a tape deck doing under the front seat?" he asked. "Why was the defendant wearing gloves and glasses? Don't you get the feeling he was staking out the liquor store?" The prosecutor stood still. He lowered his voice to a stage whisper. "Don't you get the feeling he was about to rob it? Wasn't that just like the day before when he was hanging around the parking lot behind the pet shop? Isn't that an MO? Isn't that the way he worked? When he was in the store asking about puppies, wasn't he really casing the place? And running away from the police like that. Doesn't that show consciousness of guilt?"

Taking the rifle once again from the clerk's desk, and holding it out in one hand, the prosecutor resumed his parade in front of the jury. "Do you really think Mrs. Drummond couldn't tell one black from another? If you were looking down the barrel of a gun, you wouldn't notice the hair on his face either."

The defender stood in front of the jury box to deliver his closing argument, emphasizing points by slapping his hand against the rail. "Now, the only direct evidence in this case is Mrs. Drummond's eye witness identification. What happened the next day only proves that Margaret Daniels thought somebody looked suspicious," he boomed. "What's so unusual about a friend leaving a hat in your car?" he asked. "Where's the evidence that a .22 rifle was used in the holdup? Where's the prosecutor's case? The only direct evidence the prosecutor has is Mrs. Drummond's identification, but look carefully at that. She was looking into the sunlight. The robber was wearing a long coat and a hat down below his ears.

"The prosecutor is asking you to speculate," he concluded. "But there's no room for speculation at a trial. The burden of proof is on the prosecutor. Willie is innocent until the prosecutor proves he is guilty beyond a reasonable doubt."

The defender sounded eloquent to me, and the jurors seemed attentive, although I couldn't believe they'd vote to acquit. Willie *looked* too guilty. Everyone thought so — the policemen, the prosecutor, even his own lawyer. No, he didn't think Willie was guilty of holding up Mrs. Drummond, but he thought Willie was guilty of something, and perhaps that was all that mattered.

Willie seemed to have been marked from the beginning. Guilt seemed somehow tied to his being rather than to what he was supposed to have done. But if that were true, what was the point of the trial?

That had been the week before, although it seemed much longer. The jury had hung up ten to two for conviction — a victory for Willie when the odds were better than two to one that the vote against him would be unanimous. But that had been the week before, and now there was such anger between Willie and his lawyer. With purposeful strides, the defender walked into the judge's office. He returned. He bent down. He whispered to Willie and his mother, then went back to the judge's office, clearly a messenger. Willie wasn't in court to agree to a date for a new trial. I was sure the defender was sealing a bargain and Willie was about to plead.

Mrs. Monroe confirmed my suspicion when she sat down beside me after the negotiations were over. A few minutes later the judge was at his desk, and Willie was standing beside the defender, waiving his right to the second jury trial. He told the judge, no, no one had threatened to hurt him if he didn't plead. He listened to the judge say he was letting Willie off easy because he had no prior record. He listened to the clerk read the terms of agreement: second degree robbery, three more months in jail, five years probation with intensive supervision . . .

"Five years probation! That lawyer didn't say anything about probation!" Mrs. Monroe grabbed my arm. "He said Willie should plead because he was going to be that long in jail anyway waiting for a new trial, and maybe the next time around he'd be convicted of first degree robbery, and where'd he be then. Willie kept saying no, he didn't want to say he did it when he didn't. But that lawyer talked us both down."

There were tears in Mrs. Monroe's eyes. "If I'd known about probation, I'd never have agreed to it. The police hounding him for five years." She clutched the cross at her neck. "Some lawyer," she finally said. She sounded tired. "He's just too busy for poor folk like us. He just wants to wrap everything up in a little bundle so he can get on to his big new job." She was gazing ahead at the flag on the back wall, at it or past it, I couldn't tell. "Six hundred dollars," she murmured so softly I wasn't sure she intended me to hear. "Willie would have done better with the public defender."

2

Calendar Court

They came to face the judge. Every day it was the same. The judge droned out the catechism, lawyers gave rote replies, accused robbers and burglars and murderers passed by. Their constant movement made everything dissolve and fuse into a series of surrealistic patterns: on high, the black robe silhouetted against red and white stripes; below, a blur of dark skin and white muslin.

The session always began with the players off stage, with the judge in his office, with prisoners in a stairwell behind a locked door, while mothers and wives and sweethearts took seats in the spectators' section and waited for a glimpse of their men.

Lawyers entered. A deputy district attorney came down the aisle and sat at the lawyers' table, away from the prisoners' door. An assistant public defender carried a box of files to his seat at the other end. Defense lawyers filled chairs lined up for them inside the bar. They spilled into the seats in the jury box, engrossed in their conversations. They stopped at the bailiffs' table to joke, and at the clerk's desk to gossip. They flowed into the judge's office with smiles and out again with cups of coffee.

A bailiff announced that court was in session, the hum subsided, and the judge entered, walking quickly to the platform and up two steps to his desk.

34

Calendar court is an administrative court where defendants are arraigned and assigned to other courtrooms for trial. It is where the flow of felons through the courthouse is metered. A lawyer had advised me to sit in on the proceedings to get oriented before covering any more trials. I'd done so several times, observing, noting all the details, writing everything down.

I saw about fifty defendants pass through each day. Most of them were young black men from Oakland or Berkeley. There were Chicanos from south county too, and there were some whites, and each morning a uniformed matron led two or three women prisoners to seats in the jury box to wait for the judge. But to see women criminals, you really have to go to municipal court, where prostitutes are prosecuted, and you have to go to the suburbs if you are interested in white crime.

My last day in calendar court was like all the rest. After the judge sat down, he glanced at a daily list and then called out for Rodney Cane. The bailiff called back, "He's in custody, your honor." He went to unlock the prisoners' door. Peering into a recess, he shouted, "Cane!" and a minute later a young black man wearing a white county jail jumpsuit was at the lawyers' table to be arraigned.

Near the prisoners' door, a white lawyer and a black defendant in a white jumpsuit were opposite each other in wooden chairs, conferring quietly, whispering so the bailiffs couldn't hear. They talked awhile, and then the defendant handed the lawyer a piece of paper — I thought it was a message for a woman who had waved from the back of the room — but a bailiff stood up and reached out and said, "Sorry, that's not allowed."

A man in a red poplin jacket to my left suddenly jumped up and squeezed past me down the row. Opposite the bailiffs' table, he leaned across the bar and pointed to the bailiffs' daily list of defendants, asking why someone's name wasn't there. The bailiff shrugged, and the man returned to his seat, looking over his shoulder at the audience behind him, muttering that the person he was looking for wasn't there. He sat for a moment. He pressed up against the bar. He raised his hand and wagged a finger at the judge. But the judge didn't notice. He was talking to the deputy DA. Then he was busy on the phone. Then he was staring at the bailiff and asking for George Brown.

A lawyer squatted in the aisle and conferred with a defendant who was in the audience, free on bail. As the two men talked the lawyer smiled, making it the first time that morning I'd seen a lawyer smile at his client. Another lawyer hurried past them and crossed the bar, just as George Brown came through the prisoners' door and stood before the judge.

"Where's your attorney?" the judge asked Brown.

Brown gaped at the judge.

"Aren't you George Brown? Isn't Jones your attorney?" The judge glared at the assistant public defender who was rummaging through his files and then at one of the bailiffs who was searching through files too. The judge called the bailiff to his desk. Together they looked at Brown's file. The public defender joined them and after a moment they all shrugged. The bailiff directed the prisoner out through the prisoners' door, then returned to his table mumbling something about the sheriff's department having delivered the wrong George Brown.

Another man in a white jumpsuit stood before the judge. His lawyer started to say something, but the defendant interrupted to tell the judge he didn't like this court appointed lawyer. He wanted the judge to appoint another one. He'd been in jail for a month, but this lawyer had only been to see him once. The judge looked down over his glasses and replied, "All you have a right to is competent counsel. That's all the law requires. If we allowed the defendant to choose his own counsel we'd be flooded with such requests," and his words evaporated into the high soundproofed ceiling as the defendant left by the prisoners' door.

The judge called out, "Juanita Rosario," and a woman wearing a pink blouse called back from the audience to ask if Juanita could come home from jail. "There's illness in our family and no one to care for the children," the woman told the judge. "We live in the country. There's no trouble for Juanita to get into," she implored.

"She'll find trouble if she wants to," the judge snapped, and the woman was silent. Juanita—slender, with round eyes—sat rigidly beside the matron in the jury box. A lawyer behind her continued to read his morning paper; the one beside him got up and walked down the aisle, searching the audience, looking to either side, calling for the client he was to represent that day whom he'd never met. The man in the red poplin jacket sitting beside me raised his hand and wagged a finger at the judge.

A white prisoner came before the judge to plead guilty to a drug charge. The judge told him he would have to spend a year in jail. Did he understand that he had a right to a trial, the judge asked him. Had his attorney explained that he didn't have to plead, that he had a right to take his case before a jury? Laughter was issuing from the jury box where a lawyer with a bushy moustache and one with a cigarillo dangling from his lips were talking. A deputy DA in brown and an assistant public defender in a ruffled skirt were near the bar arguing. "Has anyone threatened you?" the judge asked the prisoner as the clerk readied for the formal reading of the charges and a probation officer shuffled sheets of pink paper and a woman in the audience kissed a baby who'd begun to cry. Looking to my left, I saw that the man in the red poplin jacket was gone.

Watching the defendants filing by, I wondered who these people were and what had brought them to court. Was the man supposed to have sold drugs to support his habit, or to get rich? Had the robber boldly brandished the knife at his victim, or had his voice quavered when he demanded the money? Every prisoner I saw made me think of Willie Monroe. I had the strange sensation of being at a graduation ceremony, or even at some tribal rite of passage. The insistent footsteps on the carpeted floor had an eerie beat.

A young black man left his seat in the spectators' section to go before the judge, and he pleaded guilty to something, I wasn't able to hear what it was. The judge told him he would have to spend sixty days in jail, and the man began emptying his pockets. He was wearing a gray hooded sweat jacket. There was a hole in the back.

A short man with processed hair stood beside his lawyer in front of the judge who was pointing to a pink piece of paper, saying the man had done something wrong and was going to have his probation revoked. The bailiff unlocked the prisoners' door and as the short man left, a tall man entered and heard the judge revoke his probation for failing to report for urine tests. The tall man left, and a fat man came in, and the fat man left, and an older man came in, and a young man whose hair was still in braids.

3

The People v. Jonah Kay

Jonah Kay, also known as Jonah Dee, had been around. He had
been around for twenty years, around the bars on lower Broadway in
Oakland or south of Market in the city, where day old smoke and
vaporized alcohol wafted out into the street with the tinny music. He
had a record to show for it, a record that stretched from here to
there: Using drugs. Selling drugs. Larceny. Theft. Forgery. One
thing after another. Hardly a year went by that Jonah Kay wasn't in
some kind of hassle with the law.

The latest charge was armed robbery. When the police arrested
him in the bar on lower Broadway, he told them he couldn't have
done it. He'd been in the hospital, he said. The police winked and
smiled, knowing he was guilty, but they checked out the alibi
anyway, and found it wasn't true. It wasn't the hospital. I was
somewhere else, Kay pleaded, but the judge set bail at $14,000, and
Kay waited in county jail for three months, in maximum security,
where prisoners blew kisses to their wives and babies through thick
windows.

The first time I saw him was the day his case finally came to trial,
the day the sheriff's deputy delivered him to the courthouse jail and
the bailiff delivered him in fresh red corduroy pants and a plum-

colored shirt to the courtroom. Wandering in, knowing nothing about the case, I found Jonah Kay sitting alone at the lawyers' table, twisting his short black hair, stroking his goatee, jogging his knee up and down.

Since the whole spectators' section was mine, I took a seat in the front row near the bailiff's desk. I was saying something to the bailiff when the door to the judge's office swung open, and a tall slender man in his twenties, looking quite dashing in a bushy red moustache, a blue pinstripe suit and a bold floral tie, approached the lawyers' table with a springy step. I realized he was an assistant public defender I'd seen in calendar court.

Immediately behind him was the prosecutor, also in his twenties, a short, studious looking man with pallid skin, who walked, slightly stooped, with a plodding deliberate gait as if he carried a burden. He sat at his end of the lawyers' table, ripped a long sheet of yellow lined paper from a pad, and drew his pen back and forth, back and forth, making a thick line down the margin.

Thirty-five prospective jurors burst into the courtroom through the rear double doors, filling the seats in the spectators' section, their chattering shattering the stillness. The bailiff jumped when the buzzer by his desk sounded over the din. He disappeared into the judge's office and reappeared with a bundle of manila files, which he placed on the judge's desk.

"Court is in session," the bailiff called out, and everyone rose as the judge made his entrance with giant steps, his robe swishing back and forth and then billowing out as though he was passing over an air jet. A middle aged man whose deep tan gave him the look of someone fresh off the golf course, the judge gathered the robe about him before ascending the platform and settling into his chair.

The procession seemed oddly rehearsed, as did the action that followed. The judge squinted down at the men at the lawyers' table and then out at the audience. He said that in our democracy there was no higher duty than jury duty. He introduced the defendant as "Jonah Kay also known as Jonah Dee," casting his words out to echo in the stillness, pausing long enough to let their meaning sink in. He nodded at Jonah Kay, who forced a smile as he stood facing the audience which regarded him without expression, five black and thirty white masks, hollow eyes staring at the short stocky man with a broad nose, and age lines across his forehead, and bluish gray eyes, and mahogany skin, and an awkward space between his front teeth, and a scar on his left cheek.

The judge introduced the two lawyers. "This is the prosecutor for the people and the public defender for the defendant," he said. Then he read out the charge against Jonah Kay. "It's a serious charge," he told the jury panel. "It's a felony. The defendant says he's innocent. That will be up to the jury to decide."

The judge nodded at the clerk, and the clerk swore the jury panel in. Then the clerk cranked a cylindrical container bolted to his desk, pulled out slips of paper, and began calling out names. One by one, twelve women and men moved from the audience to the jury box.

"Now, we're going to be asking you all questions. I will. So will counsel," the judge told the twelve panelists. "We call it *voir dire.* We don't want to be nosy," he grinned, "but we have to be sure we choose a jury everyone thinks will be fair. Now, the attorneys may excuse you without giving any reason at all, and that's perfectly all right. They each get ten free challenges. And I may excuse you if there's a legal reason, if there's cause. Now, none of this is personal. You must understand that. Everyone's just doing their duty." Panelists bobbed their heads up and down.

The judge began with his list of questions typed on a piece of paper he handed to the bailiff, who passed it along to the older white woman in chair number one. The older white woman looked in her pocketbook, pulled out her glasses, read the questions, then looked up at the judge to reply. "I live in San Leandro. My husband's with the Navy. No, I don't know anyone connected with this case. I can be fair." The judge nodded, and the older white woman gave the list to a younger white woman in seat number two who said she lived in the suburb of Livermore where she was a clerk, she didn't know anyone connected with the case, and, yes, she was sure she could be fair. The judge nodded, and the younger white woman passed the list to the middle aged black man on her left. He was one of two blacks then in the jury box.

Jury selection took two and a half hours. The judge had to excuse a man for cause, a white man from San Lorenzo who insisted he couldn't be fair. The prosecutor used four of his challenges. He excused the middle aged black man, a black nurse, a Chicana teacher's assistant, and a retired white social worker. The defender used only one challenge, excusing a white woman whose husband worked in the district attorney's office and was friends with the judge. With the exception of a black dietician from the Berkeley school system, the final jury was white.

"Jeremy Tyson?" the prosecutor asked his first witness.

"Yeah."

"Jeremy, can you tell the jury where you were last December 28th, Sunday the twenty-eighth; where were you that afternoon?"

"I was visiting my father," Jeremy Tyson replied. He was eighteen or so, six feet tall, and he wore a wrinkled shirt and a scraggly beard two shades lighter than his straight brown hair. He squirmed a lot when the prosecutor began questioning him, and he shrugged his shoulders.

"And where does your father live?" the prosecutor asked him.

"Eleventh Street," Tyson replied.

"What time did you leave your father's?"

"I'm not sure." Tyson swallowed the words.

"About what time?"

"About four o'clock."

"And where did you go?"

"To the bus stop."

"Did you stop off somewhere first?"

"Yeah."

"Where?"

"Gordon's liquor store. I bought a candy bar."

"And where is Gordon's liquor store?"

"Broadway." I could barely hear the reply.

The prosecutor looked perturbed. He asked Tyson how much money he gave the clerk.

Tyson said he gave the clerk a five dollar bill.

The prosecutor asked him what he did with the change.

Tyson said he put it in his pants pocket.

"And when you got outside? What happened then?"

"I rested against the iron railing." Tyson sounded tired and he looked hot. He blew air onto his face, and he brushed the back of his hand across his forehead, even though the courtroom was chilly.

It would have been chilly that Sunday afternoon. The sun would have been low in the sky. There would have been alcoholics — winos the newspapers called them — bristly men weaving down the street, although on a Sunday afternoon there wouldn't have been many. Jeremy Tyson would have been pretty much alone.

"Did something happen when you were outside Gordon's liquor store?" the prosecutor asked.

"Two black males came up behind me," Tyson answered.

"Did these two men do something?"

"Yeah," Tyson replied.

"Can you tell the jury what it was?"

"I felt something hard poking in the back of my neck," Tyson said.

"What did you think it was?" the prosecutor asked.

"A gun," Tyson replied.

"Did someone say something?" the prosecutor asked.

"There was a voice saying he was going to kill me," Tyson said. Tyson said he couldn't see that man's face, but he could see the second man who was on his left side, reaching around to grab the four dollar bills out of his right pants pocket. The prosecutor had Tyson get up and show the jury how it happened, with Tyson playing the robber, standing to the prosecutor's left and reaching around into the prosecutor's pants pocket. "The man's face was so close it was only an inch or two away," Tyson said, and he bent down and put his face close to the prosecutor's. "I could smell the wine on his breath, and I could see his eyes." Off the stand, his speech was animated. He was easier to hear.

"Were you frightened?" the prosecutor asked when Tyson was back in his seat.

"Yeah," Tyson replied, but then his voice was so lacking in expression I wondered if he were well.

"Did you see the man who threatened to kill you?"

"I didn't get a good enough look. No, I couldn't hardly see him," Tyson said dully.

"What did the man who took the money look like?" the prosecutor asked.

"Stocky," Tyson replied.

"How tall would you say he was?"

"He came up to my ear," Tyson said.

"Where exactly? Could you show the jury?"

"Up to here." Tyson pointed to the middle of his ear.

"So he was what, five seven?"

"I guess." Tyson shrugged.

"Was there hair on his face?"

"Yeah," Tyson replied.

"Could you describe it?"

"He had a moustache." Tyson traced a line above his upper lip.

"Did he have a beard?" the prosecutor asked.

"Yeah, he had a goatee," Tyson replied.

"Was there anything you noticed about his eyes?"

"Yeah," Tyson replied.

"What was it you noticed about his eyes?"

"They were funny looking, sort of greenish blue. Yeah, they were strange. I'll never forget the eyes," Tyson told the prosecutor. From the tone of his voice, you would have thought he was telling him the time of day.

"Do you see the man who took your money here in court today?" the prosecutor asked, stepping back, away from the jury.

"Yeah." Tyson pointed at Kay.

Tyson said the two men went on down the street after they took his money. The other man, the one who threatened him, was staggering, and he was carrying an automobile antenna, which Tyson realized was what he had earlier mistaken for a gun at the back of his neck. He said he followed the two men for a short distance, but then he lost them, and he went to the police station to report the robbery.

He said he went to visit his father again on January 22nd. About a block from the bus stop he saw a man he was sure was the robber going into the Houston Bar. Since Tyson wasn't wearing his glasses at the time, he followed the man in to take a closer look. He saw him sitting on a stool in the rear. Certain of his identification, he called the police.

"When did the police arrive?"

"I don't know," Tyson shrugged.

"Did you see how many there were?"

"I seen two."

"What did they do?"

"They went in the bar, and they brought the man out."

"Did the man say anything?"

"Yeah, he said, 'It couldn't have been me because I was in the hospital.' "

"Did you give the police a description of the robber?"

"Yeah."

"What did you say?"

"I said he was stocky." Tyson shrugged.

The prosecutor said he had no more questions. The judge leaned forward to say something to the clerk, the black cloth of his sleeve hanging down from his elbow, making his arm look like a huge wing. Tyson stared glumly ahead. He seemed lost in memories of his ordeal. I couldn't help smiling at the image of him standing in the middle of the sidewalk, a robber poking an automobile antenna in his back. I noticed the bailiff staring at me, and I hastily looked down and pretended to read through my notes, telling myself it was no laughing matter. I thought of how Tyson had shuddered when he'd testified, and how he'd hunched up his shoulders. I realized that there had been times when I'd hunched up my shoulders too, trying to push away dark memories of being made to perform. There was a thin line between being the star witness and being on trial.

"Jeremy, do you have diabetes?" It was the defender.

"Yeah."

"How long have you had it?"

"I guess since I was fifteen."

"Do you take insulin for it?"

"Yeah."

"Did you take insulin on the 28th?"

"Yeah."

"Can you remember what time?"

"I guess about eight o'clock."

"Did the doctor tell you anything about eating candy?"

"He said eat it now and then."

"Did he tell you to eat it when you feel bad?"

"I don't remember."

The defender was pacing back and forth and smiling a lot, friendly smiles, not sneers. Tyson was staring at him blankly, answering mechanically.

"Does your diabetes ever affect your vision?"

"Yeah."

"Can you tell us how?"

"Sometimes I have double vision. Things get blurred."

"Were things blurred on December 28th?"

"I don't think so."

"Can you tell us what the clerk in the liquor store looked like?"

"No."

"What about the liquor store, can you describe it?"

"I don't remember."

The defender sighed. "When did you first see the robber?" he asked, lowering his voice to just above a whisper, as if he wanted Tyson's voice to sound louder, as if he wanted Tyson to make a better showing on the stand.

"I don't know, they were just suddenly behind me."

"Where did they come from?"

"I don't remember." Tyson couldn't remember anything unusual about the robber's teeth either, and he couldn't describe the other man.

"But didn't you testify at the preliminary examination that the other man weighed 160 or 170 pounds?" the defender asked, referring to the time when the prosecution had presented its case before a municipal court judge who had then decided that there was enough evidence to warrant going to trial.

"I don't remember nothing about him," Tyson replied.

"Didn't you say at the preliminary examination that the robber was twelve to fifteen inches away from you?" the defender asked.

"I don't remember."

"Look at this photo," the defender said, approaching Tyson. "Is that a picture of Mr. Kay?"

Tyson examined it for a second. "I don't know," he said.

"Did the robber have hair on his face?"

"Yeah, he had a goatee."

"Didn't you testify at the preliminary hearing that he didn't have a goatee?"

Tyson shrugged, and he shrugged some more when the defender asked him about telling the police he hadn't seen the robber's eyes.

"Do you remember what the defendant was wearing the day he was arrested?"

"Red pants."

"What about a hat?"

"I don't remember."

"But at the preliminary examination didn't you say that all you remembered about his clothing was the hat?"

"It just came to my mind that the pants he's wearing now are the same as when he was arrested."

The defender said he had no more questions and sat down, leaving

Jeremy Tyson looking forlorn on the stand. At Willie Monroe's trial, Mrs. Drummond had glossed over the flaws in her identification with self-assurance and respectability. Tyson had stumbled so. Who had taken his money? A man wearing a hat? A man wearing a goatee? I didn't see how the jury could possibly tell. There was little to go on except the witness's demeanor.

Before the judge excused Tyson, the prosecutor had one more question. "Is it difficult for you to articulate what you've seen?" he asked.

"No," Tyson replied, blinking.

"Why would Kay have lied to the police about being in the hospital if he wasn't guilty?" the prosecutor asked me. We were in the spectators' section. He was slumped in his chair, gazing at the ceiling as everyone else made ready to go home. His second, and last, witness had been Sergeant Montez who'd said Kay claimed to be in the VA hospital on December 28th, but Montez had checked and found Kay was in the hospital on December 14th, and then again on January 18th, but not on December 28th.

"Maybe Kay was confused," I offered.

"Yeah, maybe." The prosecutor didn't seem to be impressed.

"Well, maybe he *did* lie, but maybe it was because he was scared."

The prosecutor shot me a dirty look. "How many blacks do you know who have blue eyes?" he asked me.

I couldn't think of anyone. I didn't answer. There was an awkward pause. "Are you really convinced Kay is guilty?" I finally asked.

"No," he answered casually. "But that's up to the jury to decide. I'm presenting the best case I can. That's my job. My boss was just down watching Tyson testify. Oh, my god!" The prosecutor threw his hands up and laughed. "I can't control how the witness'll be on the stand. Maybe if I'd known beforehand. But my boss said as long as it's gone this far, might as well go all the way."

"Will you ask for the maximum conviction?"

"Sure."

Outside, I stood for awhile watching afternoon shadows play on the fat white courthouse tower. I thought about how Willie Monroe had pleaded guilty because a defender was too busy to go to trial. I wondered if Jonah Kay was standing trial simply because a prosecutor had to do a job.

The tower looked like an enclosure for a huge machine which I imagined churning out a procession of faceless forms.

I was haunted by the notion that two men were on trial—a lying black man and an inarticulate white man. I wasn't sure who was the villain.

The trial was delayed until eleven o'clock the next morning because the judge had an appointment. Arriving early, I found Kay and the bailiff in place, and I was just sitting down when a tiny, matronly woman pushed through the double doors at the rear of the room and came tiptoeing down the aisle with a flock of children behind her. The children filed into the seats, all whispers and giggles, and the woman pattered down to the first row to ask me what was going on. She explained that the children were sixth graders from south county, here because of a federally funded program to foster appreciation for the American legal system. She said she and the children had been looking for a trial all morning. A bailiff in another courtroom had told them to come here.

When I told her the trial was supposed to resume in a few minutes, she smiled and deposited her coat on the chair next to mine. She propped herself up on the railing, making herself taller than the children.

"All right, children. Children!" she called out over whispering that was about to explode into loud chattering. "Can someone tell me what a robbery is?"

No answer.

"Can someone tell me what an assault is?" She was looking over the first two rows of children at a little girl in the back, but still there was no answer. Children were wiggling, standing, stretching, peering out the glass panels in the doors.

"Children! What are some ways we have to prove a person committed a crime?"

Up went a hand belonging to a freckle faced girl.

"Yes, Debby?"

"Evidence."

"Good!" The teacher beamed.

All the while Jonah Kay sat at the lawyers' table, his back to the audience.

By then the lawyers and the clerk had arrived, and the judge finally emerged from his office and took a few steps to his seat. He swiveled around to the left to examine a manila file and then back again to look out at the audience. "All right, children," he said. "This is a courtroom. If you're chewing gum, get rid of it now. And don't stick it under the seat." There was a rustling, and then it was quiet again. "All right. Now, I'm the judge. This is the clerk. That's the court reporter..." One by one he introduced everybody in the case, everybody, that is, except Jonah Kay.

Dr. Judith Davidson was the first witness for the defense. She told the jury that Tyson's need for candy on the afternoon of the twenty-eighth might have meant that he'd taken an overdose of insulin, in which case he might have been confused, perhaps even intoxicated.

No sooner had she left the courtroom than a man with long side-burns came in. He walked directly to the clerk's desk. He said he was Mario Bruno. He raised his hand. He swore to tell the truth. He took the stand. Bruno told the jury he owned Gordon's liquor store. He said he didn't sell candy bars, but even if he did, his store wasn't open on Sunday afternoons. He said he knew Jonah Kay, hadn't seen him for about six months. Then the defender showed him the same photograph he'd earlier shown Tyson. Bruno said it was a picture of a man everyone called Digger who was always hanging around his store.

Digger? I put a question mark by his name in my notebook. I recalled that the defender had asked Tyson if the man in the photo looked like Kay, and Tyson had said he didn't know.

Officer Gray of the San Francisco police was the third witness for the defense. He testified that on the evening of December 27th Jonah Kay had been badly beaten by a man brandishing a lead pipe, that he had spent several hours in the hospital getting treated for bruises around his eyes and on his scalp and leg.

A day before the robbery? I jotted down. I had to write quickly because the witnesses were coming so fast: Why didn't Tyson see the bruises?

After Officer Gray, an enormous man with a long black beard and very dark skin came limping down the aisle. I guessed he was a longshoreman, but after he got to the stand he said he used to be a boxer. His name was Raymond Scott. He'd seen Jonah Kay on the twenty-ninth.

The defender asked him if Kay had been limping when he saw him, and just as Scott was opening his mouth to say yes, the prosecutor jumped up and objected. When the judge mumbled, "sustained," the defender turned red and demanded a conference at the bench. Everyone had to wait for a moment before the defender, still red, thanked and excused Mr. Scott.

If Jonah Kay was limping, why didn't Tyson notice it? I wrote. Pausing to reflect on my question, I realized another man was coming to the stand.

This tall and lanky man was an investigator in the public defender's office. He said he'd delivered a subpoena to a man named Leroy Ames ordering him to testify for the defense, and he explained that his investigation had unearthed a man named Digger who hung around bars on lower Broadway, who was about forty and who had mahogany-colored skin and bluish hazel eyes. . . .

"How the hell did this ever get so far?" the bailiff cried out. The jury had gone upstairs, and the lawyers were with the judge in his office, leaving the bailiff and Jonah Kay alone behind the bar. "I can't believe it!" He covered his ears with his hands. "A four dollar robbery? It's wild, man! Off the wall!" The bailiff leaned back in his chair and put his feet on his desk, giggling. Jonah Kay smiled wanly.

"I noticed you here yesterday," Kay said to me.

"Yes. I'm a reporter," I told him.

"Oh, who for?"

"I freelance. I write for local papers."

"You're going to write about *this* trial?" the bailiff broke in. He started laughing again before I had a chance to answer.

"You know," Kay told me, "this is like something out of Kafka. Have you read *The Trial*?"

I told him I had.

"I can't believe I'll be convicted, but with a jury like this one you can never tell."

"You've been in jail three months?"

Kay nodded. "I've been entombed."

"But they got you a lawyer right away."

"Well, for the preliminary hearing."

"Do you like your lawyer?"

"Oh, yeah, he's fine." He nodded knowingly. "He's a smart guy. He's really done his homework. Even if I could pay, I don't think a private lawyer would do better." Kay looked down for a moment. "When my wife found out I'd been arrested, she was furious," he told me. There was a gleam in his eye. " 'Who'd dare think my old man'd waste his time on this kid stuff, four lousy dollars!' She was screeching. It blew her mind. If I did something, it'd be more sophisticated," he hastened to explain. He told me that some years ago he'd embezzled a lot of money from the company he worked for. He said it was to support his habit.

The bailiff scrutinized his fingernails and chuckled to himself.

"Why *are* you covering this trial, of all things?" Kay asked me.

"No particular reason. I just wandered in. I want to see what ordinary trials are like, how the courts really work. All you ever read about are the sensational trials."

"Well, you've come to the right place," the bailiff said. "What do you live on?" he asked me, grinning.

"Faith." I laughed.

"You know, you should write about the county jail. Man, that's a bad place. Especially for whites," Kay said.

"Yeah," the bailiff chimed in. He was leaning on his elbows. "Some kid gets caught with a joint and gets sent up for a couple of days and gets raped right off the bat. He's too scared to tell. The politicians visit once a year, and they check to see if the toilets flush."

"Yeah," Kay agreed. "The kids are sitting around. There's nothing to do except wait, wait for your trial, wait to go to prison, wait to go home. There's always a fight. It relieves the tension. Just the other day there was a pretty bad fight."

"Do you feel in any sort of danger?" I asked Kay.

"Me? Oh, no." He cocked his head. "The kids sort of look up to me. I'm the old man, I've been around. I've got somewhat of a reputation, you know... It'd be different, though, in prison," he said.

"Last December 28th I was in San Francisco for the whole day and that night too," Jonah Kay said, responding to the defender's first question. He was wearing the same red pants and plum colored shirt he'd worn earlier, but something bothered me about his appearance. I couldn't figure out what it was until I realized his beard was gone.

"Mr. Kay, have you ever been in the service?" the defender was asking.

"Yes. I was in the army in 1952 — 1952 to 1954."

"And were you convicted of a felony in 1972?"

"Yes, I was. I was convicted for furnishing narcotics. I pleaded guilty. They sent me to the state hospital drug program."

Kay had gone upstairs for lunch, and now he was back in the courtroom, on the stand, and he looked different because his beard was gone! Tyson had testified that the robber wore a goatee. What were the jurors to think except that Kay had tried to shave away his resemblance to the robber?

"Before that where did you work?"

"In Detroit. I was a computer programer. I was making $36,000 a year."

"And after you were released from the state hospital what did you do?"

"I started a drug program in Oakland. We got federal funds."

"Now, Mr. Kay. This morning you had a beard, and this afternoon you don't. Could you explain to the jury why that is?" Finally. So long as the question was left there dangling, it was almost impossible to take seriously what Kay was saying.

"Black people use a special kind of depilatory for shaving," Kay said, sounding somewhat like a school teacher. "I was getting ready to testify after lunch, and I put too much depilatory on, and it made a lopsided beard, so I shaved the whole thing off."

"And can you tell the jury now if you are presently in any sort of medical treatment?" the defender asked.

"Yes. I'm presently in treatment for hypertension." Kay said he'd been in the hospital in December and then again in January. He'd been in and out of the hospital so many times he'd forgotten precisely when it was. "I spent the last three months writing letters and searching my memory to reconstruct my life over all of December."

"And can you tell the jury now where you were on December 27th, the Saturday before the robbery?"

"Yes. It was in the evening, and I was in the Mission District in San Francisco, and I saw these two men attacking a woman, and I went to help her. One of the men hit me with a lead pipe."

"Were you badly hurt?"

"Well, it was pretty bad. He hit me in my right knee, and that's my trick knee."

"And how did you get a trick knee?"

"From playing college football."

College football, damsels in distress. I was writing it all down.

"After you were hit, what happened?"

"The police came. I went in the ambulance to the city hospital. It was two in the morning before I got out. There weren't any more buses to Oakland, so I stayed with a friend downtown."

"What was your friend's name?"

"Leroy Ames." Kay said he spent all of Sunday with Ames too, and Sunday night. He said he got home Monday morning to have lunch with his wife.

"And what is your wife's name?"

"Janet. Janet Smiley. Her father used to be an editor for the *Los Angeles Star*."

Kay said that on January 22nd he went into the Houston Bar for cigarettes. The next thing he knew, Tyson was identifying him, and he was under arrest. "He really thought I did it."

"Do you know a man named Digger?"

"Yes, I know him in passing. He looks something like me, about the same age and the same height. His eyes are blue too. I'm a little heavier."

"Mr. Kay, did you rob Jeremy Tyson?"

Kay shook his head. "No," he said. He was meeting the jurors' stares straight on. His eyes looked bluer than before, and under the fluorescent light directly over the witness stand, his skin looked lighter.

Jonah Kay was acquitted. The jury came to its decision twenty minutes after listening to the lawyers' closing arguments and the judge's legal instructions.

Addressing the jury, the prosecutor had looked like he was about to deliver a lecture, or perhaps a sermon. He stood behind a metal lectern, which held his notes. All the jurors were attentive. One folded her hands over her purse which lay in her lap like a kangaroo's pouch. The prosecutor explained the purpose of his closing summary: to acquaint the jurors with the facts as he saw them and the law. "The defender will have his turn to argue, and I'll have a chance to rebut him. I get an extra chance because the burden of proof is on me."

He tapped his finger on the lectern. He smoothed back his hair with his hand. "All right," he said. "To begin with, Jeremy Tyson isn't a very bright person." The words shot out like swords. At that moment I saw Jeremy Tyson behind the lawyers' table sitting next to Jonah Kay. I saw the prosecutor leaving the lectern and walking up to Kay and peeling the scar off of Kay's cheek and sticking it onto Tyson's.

It was a fantasy that stayed with me long after the trial.

4

The People v. John Ramsey

He was six feet eight inches tall and he weighed 350 pounds. A conservative sports suit failed utterly to mask his size. He stood at the rear of the courtroom talking to the woman who had followed him in. When the lawyers emerged from the judge's office, he moved awkwardly down the aisle to the lawyers' table. His companion sat in the spectators' section.

"The district attorney of the county of Alameda by this amended information hereby accuses John Ramsey of a felony, to wit . . ." The judge read out the charges to the jury panel which filled the room, a list so long it seemed to twine around the defendant:

Violation of section 245b of the penal code of California, assault with a deadly weapon on Police Officer Glenn Wright;

Violation of section 12031 of the penal code of California, carrying a loaded gun in a public place;

Violation of section 12023 of the penal code of California, carrying a concealed weapon without a license;

Violation of section 245 of the penal code of California, assault with a deadly weapon on Henry Billings;

Violation of section 32 of the penal code of California, after the Billings assault, helping Marvin Washington escape arrest . . .

Marvin Washington! The words rippled through the audience, up and down rows, to the back of the room. There was murmuring, whispering, no one daring to say the black revolutionary's name out loud.

"I want this courtroom to be as free from passion and rage as a hospital room is from germs." The judge's voice broke through. "You listen to what the witnesses say. You consider the material evidence. You don't think about gossip or what you've read in the papers." He was frowning, and deep lines ran down the center of his forehead. The courtroom grew still.

No, it wasn't an ordinary trial, although I was impressed by how ordinary everyone was trying to make it seem—the judge droning on about the law, the clerk cranking her little container and picking out twelve names, the judge explaining to the jury panel how a jury was chosen and the meaning of *voir dire*. The prosecutor stood with his hands clasped in front of him when he asked a prospective juror if she would be upset at having guns placed in evidence, if she'd ever had a bad experience with the police. The defender's voice was level when he asked a prospective juror if he thought a policeman could lie, if he harbored ill will toward Marvin Washington or Washington's Commoner Movement, if he would hold John Ramsey responsible for some crime because of his association with Washington. The prosecutor and defender both excused women and men they didn't want on the jury. They smiled. They were polite. When the jury was finally chosen (all but three were white), left-over panelists filed quietly out of the courtroom, and a half a dozen of Ramsey's comrades filed silently in. Everyone seemed united in wanting to deny the excitement attached to the trial.

The first prosecution witness was Officer Glenn Wright, a big tall athletic looking man who wore an Afro haircut and a goatee and who was dressed in a light brown suit and a gold tie. He seemed at ease on the stand. Answering the prosecutor's questions, he sounded businesslike, self-assured. He frequently looked at the jury.

Officer Wright said he was a vice officer, which meant he dealt with drugs, alcohol, gambling, and prostitution. On the evening of June 24th, ten months before, he and his partner, Robert Talbott, had been in the Stanford Lounge in the Merritt Shores shopping center in Oakland, a place they went to a couple of times a week on prostitution investigation. They'd seen two prostitutes sitting at the bar, and they'd decided to stay a while to observe them. They'd also seen the defendant, John Ramsey, sitting in a booth.

The prosecutor asked Officer Wright to show the jury exactly where he'd been standing, and Wright got up and went to an easel near the jury box. Using a pointer, he pointed to a spot on a huge diagram, and he explained to the jury what everything else on the diagram was too—the thick black lines near the bottom were the cashier's booth, the ones near the top were the bandstand, the dance floor here, tables there, and the men's room. It took Officer Wright several minutes to explain the diagram. As he talked, air blew in through the vent near the ceiling, making a rapid clicking sound.

"When you first went to the Stanford Lounge, did you have any idea that Mr. Ramsey was going to be there?" the prosecutor asked.

"None whatsoever," Wright replied.

"Had you personally ever met Mr. Ramsey before?"

"No, I hadn't." Wright adjusted his tie.

"And why did Mr. Ramsey attract your attention?"

"Well, Mr. Ramsey is a large man, quite large." Wright held his hands apart. "He kind of stands out."

"Now, as a law enforcement officer did you have any information concerning Mr. Ramsey even though you had never met him?"

"I did."

"And from whom had you received that information?"

"I received that information from Agent D. D. Norton of the ATF—the Alcohol, Tobacco and Firearms unit of the U.S. Treasury Department."

"And what information did Agent Norton give to you?"

"He said . . ."

"Objection! Hearsay!" The defender jumped up.

"Objection overruled," the judge mumbled, motioning for the defender to sit, waving him still.

"Ladies and gentlemen," the judge looked down at the jury. "At this time I want to explain that the information that Mr. Wright has is not being offered for the truth of the information but only to show why Mr. Wright acted as he acted. So bear that in mind." He nodded at the prosecutor.

"Thank you, your honor." The prosecutor nodded back. "Mr. Wright, what information was it you had about Mr. Ramsey?" he asked quietly.

"He said that Mr. Ramsey was hired as a bodyguard for Mr. Marvin Washington and that Mr. Ramsey, while in the company of Mr. Washington, was always armed."

"Now, after you were standing near the booth, what did you do next?"

"Well, I didn't do anything except to continue to observe. I took up my position at the booth, looking in the direction of the prostitutes."

"Now, sometime after you noticed Mr. Ramsey, did you notice anyone else that attracted your attention?" the prosecutor asked, pursing his lips.

"I did."

"And who was that?"

"Mr. Washington, Marvin Washington."

"And where did you see Marvin Washington?"

"He was sitting at this booth here." Wright was at the easel again, using the pointer. "There's a seat that comes out, this way. Mr. Washington was sitting right here."

"Now, Mr. Wright. After you first saw Mr. Washington seated at the booth, what is the next thing you observed him do?"

"After I observed him for three or four minutes, he began staring at me, and I looked away from him. Later I saw him get up and walk over to Mr. Ramsey and whisper something to him."

"Did you notice whether or not Mr. Ramsey was holding anything?"

"Yes, I did. He was holding a black attaché case, roughly that long and about that wide." He spread his hands about two feet apart. "And he had a leather coat draped over his arm, this way . . . with the attaché case held in his left arm over his chest."

"Now, after Mr. Washington whispered something to Mr. Ramsey, what did Mr. Washington do?"

"Mr. Washington, I believe, returned to his seat for a few minutes."

"And then what did he do?"

"He got up again and came to the area of the bar and ordered a drink, and Mr. Ramsey came up and paid for the drink. He reached into the attaché case for the money."

"And after that where did Mr. Washington go?"

"He came to this area here . . . and joined some other people.

Then he got up and went back and whispered something to Mr. Ramsey."

"And Mr. Ramsey was carrying the attaché case the whole time?"

"He was."

"And what happened then?"

"Well, Mr. Ramsey went over and sat with Mr. Washington, and they had a few drinks, and Mr. Washington became quite loud, and he again leaned over and whispered something to Mr. Ramsey, and the two of them got up and went to the men's room. They stayed there about five minutes, and Mr. Washington came out, with Mr. Ramsey following him ... stops right here," pointing to the diagram, "said some goodbyes, waved at a few people. Mr. Ramsey then took the coat from his arm and draped it over Mr. Washington's shoulders and then the two of them exited the door."

"Now, after they went out, did you do anything?"

"I did."

"And what was that?"

"My partner and I got up and we also exited."

"And what happened after you got outside?"

"Mr. Washington stopped, and he turned around and said, 'Are you fucking pigs following me?' "

The prosecutor gave Wright a felt tipped pen, and he had him mark on the diagram where they all had been when Washington said that. As the pen squeaked and Wright made little red x's, the judge bent over to watch.

Wright said he told Washington, no, he wasn't following him. He said Washington replied, "I'll see if you're following me because I'm going back in." Washington went into the lounge and then he came right back out, and he said, "To show you the kind of man I am, I'll buy you a drink," and Wright replied, "To show you the kind of man I am, I'll accept your drink."

"Mr. Washington walked up to the bar, threw up both hands and said, 'Stop the music. I want to make an announcement.' "

"And was the music stopped?"

"I don't know if it was or not."

"And what happened after that?"

"He said, 'I want to buy these fucking pigs a drink.' "

"And then what happened?"

"He turned to me and he said, 'What do you drink?' "

"And what did you reply?"

" 'I drink Courvoisier.' "

"And then what happened?"

"Mr. Washington looked at me and stated, 'When you finish drinking that drink, I'm going to fuck you.' "

"Then what happened?"

"I asked him what did he mean by that."

Wright said there was more loud hollering, and he warned Washington that he could get into trouble for creating such a scene. He said Washington responded by shoving his coat off his shoulders and making a gesture (his finger for a gun) and ordering Ramsey, "Shoot him, shoot the pig ass motherfucker, shoot him!"

"Ramsey was right there next to Washington. He made a step toward me and dove his hand into his bag," Wright continued. "I drew my revolver, pointed it at Mr. Ramsey and told him to drop the bag or I would shoot him. He hesitated. He didn't move. He more or less froze. My partner walked by me—this is my partner here, this is myself, and this is Mr. Ramsey." Wright was blocking out the space with his hands. "My partner then reached out with his revolver and knocked the bag from Mr. Ramsey's hand to the floor." Wright said they found a loaded gun in the attaché case. They took Ramsey outside and put on the handcuffs. They used two pairs of handcuffs because Ramsey was so big.

Wright took up the felt tipped pen and made little red x's on the diagram to show where everyone was when Washington gave Ramsey the order, and everyone watched. "W-7 will indicate the position of Mr. Ramsey," the judge announced, and the court reporter took it down. "W-8 will be the position of Mr. Talbott."

The judge sounded so calm and unemotional I had to remind myself that I wasn't in a sterile room, as he had insisted, but that I was watching a political trial. After all, this wasn't a case of an ordinary barroom brawl. It was the case of John Ramsey, a Commoner accused of assaulting a cop. Everyone knew there was a bitter history between the Commoners and the police. If you watched TV, you knew the Commoners once openly marched with guns in defiance of the police, you knew once there was a big shootout between the two. And if you read the daily and the alternative press, you knew there had been government memos authorizing the ATF to give a hard time to militant groups, authorizing FBI agents to pin-

point troublemakers in the Commoner Movement and to "neutral-
ize" them before they exercised their potential for violence. You
knew that at least twenty Commoners had in fact been killed, and
hundreds more had been arrested. You knew that just a few months
before the Stanford incident, Oakland policemen told a reporter the
political climate was right to make a move against the Commoners.
You knew that three months after the Stanford incident, after he'd
been charged with the same assaults as Ramsey, and then a murder
too, Marvin Washington had fled to a foreign country charging the
police were bound and determined to frame him and he'd never get a
fair trial.

If you read the daily and alternative press, you knew all of that,
but how many jurors had? John Ramsey's friends and comrades
were there in the audience convinced that Officer Wright and his
partner had followed Washington out of the bar in a deliberate
attempt to provoke him, and the prosecutor stood on the other side
convinced that he was pitted against a dangerous, vicious man. But
the jurors were hearing calm voices and clicking air vents and
squeaking pens. They were hearing a bureaucratic rendition of a
political trial.

When he cross examined Officer Wright, the defender paced back
and forth, gesturing a lot, his voice animated. Still, he seemed helpless to break the sterile seal.

"D. D. Norton was working as an agent with the Oakland police
department to watch militant groups, is that correct?" the defender
asked.

"I don't know what D. D. Norton's job was, sir," Wright replied.

"Well, what was he doing coming to vice control to tell about
Washington's activities?" the defender persisted.

"All agencies work together. They give us information as we do
them," Wright replied.

"Did D. D. tell you to keep watch over Mr. Washington?" the
defender asked.

"No, sir," Wright replied.

"Did he give you the impression he wanted you to do surveillance
work for the Treasury Department?" the defender asked.

"I don't work for Mr. Norton, and he can't give me any, you
know, any instructions about work surveillance of nobody," Wright
replied.

"Did you ask D. D. why he was picking you out and not telling some of the other officers?" the defender asked.

"No, I felt it was obvious why," Wright replied.

"Because you have a reputation for wanting to get Marvin Washington, is that correct?" the defender asked.

"No, I don't believe I have that reputation," Wright replied.

It wasn't that the defender's questions weren't meaningful. They certainly were. But their meaning was obscured by the mood. He asked Wright: "Didn't you know you were asking for a confrontation when you tried to defend your manhood by saying you'd let Washington buy you a drink?" But the impact of the question was dulled by the prosecutor's mumbled objection ("Argumentative, assuming facts not in evidence") and the judge's stern reply ("Mr. Prosecutor, just make your objections. Explanations aren't necessary. Mr. Defender, tighten up your questioning.") It was dulled by the faint sounds of a lawyer clearing his throat and a court reporter tapping away at his little machine.

At the beginning of the trial the judge had told the jurors their job was to decide whether or not witnesses were telling the truth. If so much of the story was going to be sanitized out, I didn't see how they could.

When Officer Talbott testified he told almost exactly the same story as Officer Wright. He was a big man and tall. He wore an Afro haircut too, and he told the story again of Washington challenging Wright to have a drink, and of Ramsey reaching for the gun, adding that Washington was loud and obnoxious, he seemed high, and he gave orders to Ramsey by snapping his fingers.

On cross examination the defender asked Talbott if he knew of any police agents inside the Commoner Movement or any wiretaps on Washington's phone.

Talbott said he didn't.

The defender asked Talbott if he was familiar with Wright's reputation for honesty and veracity.

Talbott replied, "I know my partner is an honest man."

The defender asked Talbott if he'd ever heard any reports about Officer Wright, but the prosecutor objected before the defender could explain what reports he meant, and the judge called the two lawyers over to a conference at his desk.

"Officer Talbott, would your opinion about Wright being an honest man remain if you heard reports that he had stolen something?" the defender asked when the conference was over. He was standing directly in front of the judge's desk. The prosecutor was just behind him. He was speaking slowly, as if he were waiting for the judge to approve each and every word, as if he were groping for just the right mix to remain within the law.

"Yes, my opinion would remain because . . ."

"No, just yes or no," the judge broke in.

"Okay. Yes." Talbott sounded annoyed.

"Your honor, I would ask that the jury be admonished because of the nature of the question, we are bound by certain rules of evidence," the prosecutor said softly.

"Yes." The judge looked down on the jury. "The question, ladies and gentlemen, does not prove or suggest or state that Mr. Wright has stolen anything. It is merely a question designed to go into whether or not the opinion of Mr. Talbott would be the same if he knew certain things."

"If the court pleases, usually the instructions are left . . ."

"Mr. Defender, we will get along much better if you do your job, and I will try and muddle through and do mine."

The defender sighed and went on with his questions. Juror number four looked puzzled. There was no earthly reason for her to guess that Officer Wright was once suspended from the police force because he was caught shoplifting. I knew. The defender had told me before the trial. He'd sounded terribly excited to have such damaging information about the prosecution's star witness. He'd planned to cast suspicion on Officer Wright in the same way I'd seen prosecutors cast suspicion on defendants. But I didn't think the strategy had worked. Frankly, I was sure the defender had lost the case, but that was before Harvey Miller took the stand.

Harvey Miller was a mild mannered, middle aged, regular customer at the Stanford Lounge. He'd been there on June 24th. He'd been at the bar. He'd been sitting just a few feet from where Washington and Wright were when they were arguing. He'd heard Washington call out, "The pigs are fucking with me, the motherfucking pigs are following me, the motherfucking pigs are trying to fuck me." He'd heard Officer Wright reply, "Hey, man, we're not fucking with you.

Why don't you calm down?" He'd heard Washington hollering and cursing some more, and he'd seen Officer Wright pull his revolver. He indicated he was uncomfortable repeating all those dirty words in front of the jury, but the judge told him he had to, and he sat there on the witness stand talking clearly, testifying for the prosecution.

"Now, at the time Officer Wright pulled his gun, did you see where Ramsey was?"

"Yes, I did," Miller said. "He walked, like from about the end of the bar, and I think at that point was when Officer Talbott came in and ordered Mr. Ramsey to drop his briefcase."

"And did Mr. Ramsey drop it?" the prosecutor asked.

"No, he didn't," Miller said. "Officer Talbott came over and reached out and pulled it from his arm and threw it on the floor."

The prosecutor went on with his questions, but I suddenly stopped hearing. I turned back a page in my notebook and reread my notes: "Then Officer Wright pulled his revolver," and Miller was right there, but he didn't see Ramsey even though Wright and Talbott both had said Ramsey was standing next to Washington. Nor had Miller mentioned anything about Washington ordering Ramsey to shoot Wright. Miller had said he hadn't seen Ramsey until sometime later when Ramsey was at the end of the bar, some distance from Washington who was near the center. What a bold contradiction of Wright's and Talbott's testimony by the prosecutor's own witness!

And the eerie part was that Miller had just said it, and I'd just written it down, but I didn't remember hearing it. What I remembered was "The motherfucker is a pig."

"Mr. Miller, you were at the bar when you heard the yelling, is that right?" The defender began cross examination.

"Yes," Miller replied.

"Do you recognize what I'm showing you now, people's exhibit number four?"

"I recognize it as a briefcase of sorts."

"You couldn't say if this is the same briefcase that you saw Mr. Ramsey carrying that night?"

"No, I couldn't."

"But it was similar?"

"Yes, it was similar."

"Could you describe for the court and for the jury how Ramsey was carrying his briefcase?"

"Yes, he had it . . ."

"Here, let me give you the case."

Miller took the attaché case. "He had it just like this," he said. "He had it underneath his arm like that." Miller tucked the case under his arm, way up under his armpit. If Ramsey had held the case like that, it would have been impossible for him to reach inside for a gun.

In the hallway at recess time, John Ramsey was suddenly surrounded by children, students from the Commoners' school who had been sitting silently through most of the afternoon session. One little one had slept in a teacher's arms. They were teasing Ramsey, and he was teasing back. He picked a little girl up by her elbows, lifted her high in the air. The girl squealed with delight. Elevator doors slid open, and two public defenders came out. One looked at Ramsey. He nudged the other one, whispering, "Wow! Look at his size!"

It wasn't only the political issues that were lost in this trial. John Ramsey was too. He'd been sitting silently through the testimony, a large dark form. "He kind of stands out." "Two pairs of handcuffs because he was so big." "Wow! Look at his size!" That was John Ramsey.

Henry Billings was a handsome man whose silver gray hair set off his light brown skin. He had a full moustache and thick dark eyebrows. The knit suit he wore fit him perfectly. His appearance on the witness stand marked the opening of part two of the same trial since the story he had to tell had nothing whatever to do with the fight at the Stanford Lounge. John Ramsey was on trial for two completely different crimes.

I had trouble following the beginning of Billings' testimony. It wasn't that Billings was timid or boring. At times he was something of a ham. But as he explained the kind of work he did (he was a tailor) and then described his first meeting with Marvin Washington, my mind was so crowded with images from the Stanford incident, I couldn't visualize what he was saying. He said he first met Washington at a bar. I imagined Washington and Wright at the Stanford. He said Marvin Washington invited him to his apartment where he offered him a drink. Again I saw Washington and Wright. I wished they'd separate the charges and hold two separate trials.

Actually, the defender had tried to get a judge to do just that, to order two separate trials. He'd argued that simply having so many charges lumped together could make the jury think Ramsey was guilty. But the judge had ruled against him, to no one's surprise, since there was nothing particularly unusual about Ramsey's situation. Often defendants stood trial for many charges at once — a whole string of burglaries, for instance, or a whole string of kidnappings. In one case I read about they tried together twelve defendants who were all charged with similar crimes, so many defendants that the jury was given their photographs to keep straight who they were. Lumping cases together is supposed to help the courts to run efficiently. Time would have been lost if John Ramsey had had two separate juries, if the prosecutor had made two opening arguments, if the judge had delivered his legal instructions twice. Still, my head would have been clearer if there *had* been two separate trials. Trials were supposed to give defendants a chance to confront their accusers and juries a chance to consider the evidence, or so I'd been told.

Billings continued with his testimony. Eventually the details of the Stanford incident faded, and Billings' story became vivid. I was in Washington's two bedroom apartment with picture windows and carpeted floors. I was sitting at his dining room table late one Saturday morning with Billings and Washington and Washington's brother-in-law, sipping seventeen-dollar-a-bottle cognac, joking, passing the time of day.

I became so absorbed in Billings' story I could actually see the expression on Billings' face when he told Washington he'd never enjoyed cognac so much and when Washington brought out a bottle for him to take home. I could feel the fabric samples Billings took out of his briefcase, the knits, the velvets. I could see him nod at Washington's wife who was in the kitchen — "Sweetheart, would you get me another glass, please" — and I could see Washington's eyes flash as he told Billings, "Don't call her sweetheart. I don't like that." I could feel the tension.

I could see Washington fidgeting in his chair, standing up, going to the window, returning to the table, sitting again. I could hear him saying, "I've been ripped off so many times, I want you to promise me one thing and I'll let you make my clothes. I want you to make my assistant a suit (he was referring to John Ramsey who wasn't there) and I want you to give me the same price for him and me."

"Baby, I can't give you and Mr. Ramsey the same price," Billings replied in disbelief. "Think of the size of the man!"

Baby? "Don't you call me baby!" That was what Billings said triggered it off. Washington got so mad at Billings for calling him baby that he went and got a gun and, Bam! He hit Billings on the side of the head with the butt.

"Blood started shooting out everywhere." That's what Billings told the jury. "Then I turned my head . . . like that . . . Well, I saw the blood, turned my head, and that time he hit me on the side, and I'm bleeding, blood is all in my eyes and everything. Well, when he hit me the second time he kicked the chair over, then he kicked me on the side, then he kicked me in the mouth, because I broke my partial. It broke my partial."

There was all that blood, and Billings said Washington kept right on hitting him with the pistol. "Eventually I said to myself, I said, 'Well, Jesus, the man will kill me, I better do something.' So at this point I was pretty weak, so I caught him on the jeans — he had a pair of jeans on — and I pulled myself up, and I tried to hit him, but at the same time I didn't have too much strength, and I fell on top of him, and he went against the wall. Well, he was a little bit drunk, I think the man was drunk, you know, and blood was going all over everywhere. At that point Ramsey came in."

Ramsey came in. You know, Billings had been testifying for at least twenty minutes, and in that time all he'd said about Ramsey was "the size of the man." When Billings said Ramsey's name, I was actually startled. I had to jog my memory to see the face. I tried remembering what Harvey Miller had said. I couldn't. I tried remembering what Officer Wright looked like. He looked like Henry Billings. I tried remembering the Stanford Lounge, but all I saw was Marvin Washington six feet eight inches tall coming in the front door, John Ramsey all spattered with blood. John Ramsey wasn't on trial anymore. During the course of the trial, he'd become a large dark form that stood for the absent Marvin Washington.

"Well, I passed out, I guess," Billings told the jury. "The next thing I knew, Ramsey was behind me, and Washington told him to hold me up while he was going to ask me some questions. So Washington tried to force me to say I came to his apartment and molested him, and each time I refused he would hit me with his fist, or the pistol, I don't remember."

"And who was holding you at the time Washington was hitting you?" the prosecutor asked.

"Mr. Ramsey."

The prosecutor paused, I guess because that statement was his case against Ramsey on the second assault charge. If Ramsey *had* held Billings down, he was as guilty as if he'd delivered the beating himself.

"Washington told Mr. Ramsey to take me out of there," Billings was at the end of his story. " 'Get him out of there.' And there was a little fellow too. He gave me my briefcase, and I asked for the bottle of cognac.

"They took me down the elevator to the garage, and they wanted to put me in the back seat, but Mr. Ramsey told the little fellow, he says, 'Put some paper on the back seat. I don't want blood all over my car.' And they put paper in and shoved me in the car and slammed the door. They drove me to my apartment, and they snatched me out near the garage. They threw the briefcase out after me, and they threw out the fifth of cognac."

On cross examination the defender went over what Billings had said at the preliminary hearing. He took a lot of time. He found a lot of contradictions. He tried to make it look like Billings was so beaten up and so drunk he couldn't possibly have known what was happening by the time Ramsey arrived.

But then the prosecutor got up for redirect, and he pulled a crumpled-up pinstripe suit out of a brown paper bag. He held it up and paraded back and forth, tiptoed really, in front of the jury. It was Billings' suit, and it was horribly stained. Juror number four winced and looked down at her lap. So did I.

That was the beginning of a bloody parade. The prosecutor's next witness was a Mrs. Bradley who said she saw Ramsey deliver Billings to his home. Billings had been so terribly beaten up and bleeding so profusely that she hadn't recognized him when he got out of the car. The apartment manager came next to say that she had called the ambulance, and she'd had the janitor mop up the blood from the garage floor. Then came Dr. Jones who said that Billings' skull had been shattered and his brain had been visible in one place.

One after the other, five policemen took the stand to identify items they found in Washington's apartment later that night—bloody towels, bloody carpeting, bloody jeans, a gun with a broken butt. The prosecutor passed among the jurors a stack of photographs taken at the scene. An undercover vice squad agent told how he arrested Ramsey later that evening. He said he used two pairs of handcuffs because Ramsey was so big.

The prosecutor concluded by playing a tape for the jury, a statement Billings had given the police from his hospital bed after he was beaten. On tape Billings was moaning a lot and gasping for breath, telling pretty much the same story he'd just told on the stand, except for one detail: On tape he didn't say anything about Ramsey coming in and holding him while Washington delivered the beating. I didn't know if that was important or not. With all the blood it was impossible to tell.

I think it was then that I realized that I'd been listening to the testimony with almost no feeling. There Billings had been describing how he'd received an incredible beating, and instead of pitying him I'd been eyeing him suspiciously, listening for inconsistencies in his story. Just as the prosecutor was using Ramsey as a stand-in for Washington, so he was using Billings, the blood and the gore, to plug up the loopholes in Officer Wright's story. I realized I'd been blaming Billings for what the prosecutor was doing.

At recess time the judge came out of his office and looked around the empty courtroom. He turned toward the bailiff who was on the phone. "Where's Ramsey?" he mumbled.

"Who?" the bailiff called out, putting his hand over the mouthpiece.

"Ramsey," the judge raised his voice. "You know, the short guy," he grinned.

The bailiff chuckled. "Dunno. Think he went down to the snack bar." He resumed his telephone conversation, and just as the judge disappeared into his office, Ramsey came into the courtroom.

It probably would have gone better for him if John Ramsey hadn't testified on his own behalf, but those things are always hard to tell. In taking the stand he risked making a bad impression on the jury, although by that time the prosecutor had so bloodied Ramsey's image that maybe Ramsey figured he had nothing to lose.

Ramsey testified for a long time, sitting frozen in his chair, talking slowly, as if he were listening to every word himself before letting anyone hear it. The defender had him say things like he wasn't Washington's bodyguard, and he went to college when he lived in South Carolina, things to make the jury respect him. And the defender had him talk about things like the Commoners' school and the books Marvin Washington had written, things to make the jury respect Washington.

Ramsey denied all of the charges against him. He told the jury the same version of the Stanford incident Harvey Miller had, and he denied any part in the assault on Billings. He said he arrived at Washington's apartment after the fight, and he admitted he took Billings home, but he said he offered to take Billings to the hospital (he said Billings refused) and he denied throwing Billings out of the car. He also said there was no basis to the charge that he was involved in a plan for Washington's escape. There never had been any such plan. In fact, Washington had turned himself in to the police later that night as soon as he learned there was a warrant out for his arrest.

That part of Ramsey's testimony went smoothly. It was helpful being reminded of what had happened at the Stanford Lounge. But there were also things that Ramsey said that sounded to me like lies, and after he said them I don't think that anything else mattered.

He said that no one else had been in the car with him and Billings when he took Billings home, which contradicted not only Billings' testimony but Mrs. Bradley's. Mrs. Bradley had said there were at least two men with Billings in the car. I couldn't imagine why she would have lied.

Then, a little later, when Ramsey was under cross examination, the prosecutor caught him in what was clearly another lie:

"Have you ever fired a gun in Oakland?" the prosecutor asked him.

"No," Ramsey said he hadn't.

"You've never fired a gun in Oakland?" the prosecutor asked.

"No." Ramsey was insistent.

"On November 22nd, 1971, on the corner of Fourth and Acacia, you didn't fire a gun?" the prosecutor asked. He was reading from a xeroxed sheet of paper I assumed was a police report, and Ramsey seemed suddenly flustered.

"Oh, yes," Ramsey said, "once I *did* shoot a gun in Oakland."

The worst came at the very end when the prosecutor asked Ramsey if he'd returned to Washington's apartment after taking Billings home and Ramsey denied it:

"You didn't get into the elevator with Washington and Washington's wife around four o'clock that afternoon?" the prosecutor asked him.

"No, I didn't," Ramsey replied.

"So there is no confusion, Mr. Ramsey, the date is July 20th, the place is 150 Wildcreek Drive," the prosecutor told him.

"I understand that," Ramsey replied.

The prosecutor ran his fingers across his lips, then went to his chair. After the noon recess he introduced Raymond D'Arcy, his rebuttal witness, a timid gray-haired man who said he was a janitor in Washington's apartment house. D'Arcy said that on July 20th at four o'clock in the afternoon he'd been cleaning the blood off the carpet outside Washington's apartment when Ramsey and Washington and Washington's wife came out and got into the elevator.

"A witness willfully false in one material part of his testimony is to be distrusted in the others"—that's what the judge in Willie Monroe's trial had told the jury. That's what this judge would tell this jury too. And it wouldn't have to matter why John Ramsey said what he did—to cover his tracks? to protect a friend? to make the jury like him? He'd be a liar.

Ramsey on the stand reminded me of Willie Monroe—the flaws in Mrs. Drummond's story, Willie's prosecutor parading back and forth with the rifle, the scar suddenly so prominent on Willie's brown face, Ramsey's face, Marvin Washington's face scarred by lies.

Was John Ramsey guilty or innocent of the charges against him? The question was lost in bureaucratic procedure. And I wasn't sure it was what the trial ever had been about.

The jury came down with the verdicts two days later. The foreman announced that the jurors hadn't been able to agree on the assault charge against Billings, but they'd agreed on all the rest. The clerk read out the verdicts: "Guilty" on the two gun charges; "Guilty" of helping Washington try to escape arrest; "Guilty" of assault on Wright. The last one puzzled me since the jury found Ramsey guilty of simple assault against the police officer, not assault with a gun, which meant he'd somehow threatened Officer Wright but he hadn't reached into his briefcase. I couldn't remember any evidence to support such a verdict. After the jury left, some of us who had been observing the trial stayed on to chat. We decided the jury must have been badly split, and the verdicts must have represented compromises. A lawyer said compromise verdicts were common.

That night I decided to telephone jurors to see if we were right. I reached one black juror who didn't want to talk about the trial and several white jurors who were reticent too, but I finally reached Anthony Lawrence, a middle aged white salesman from the suburb of Livermore who answered my questions quite willingly.

He told me he'd enjoyed being on the jury. He said he thought it was educational, and everyone had tried to be fair. "We couldn't agree on the Stanford assault," he told me. "There were a sufficient number of people who listened to Harvey Miller. But we agreed on the lesser charge—simple assault—because Ramsey kept walking after Wright warned him to stop, and that could have been considered menacing by the police officer."

"Didn't Ramsey claim he didn't hear Wright?" I asked.

"Yes, I know." Lawrence said that had bothered the jury too, but "We had to discount that because we weren't there. We wanted to go to the bar to see the lighting and to hear the noise level. We asked for measurements. But the judge said we couldn't."

"If the defender had been allowed to show that Wright was once suspended from the police department because he was caught shoplifting, would that have made a difference?"

"I don't know. That's hard to say." Mr. Lawrence didn't sound particularly surprised. "There still would have been Talbott's testimony," he said.

I asked him what the jury had thought about the Billings assault. He told me there were two jurors who weren't convinced. They thought Billings was beaten too badly to remember what happened. So the jury hung up there.

"But you agreed Ramsey was trying to conceal the crime?" I asked him.

"Yes," he replied. "Ramsey took Billings home, and the most glaring thing was that the man was seriously hurt, but Ramsey didn't get him medical help or ask what happened."

"Did it make any difference that Ramsey was a Commoner?"

"No, not really. Some of the women were edgy, I guess. They asked the bailiff who all the people in the audience were, and he said he wasn't allowed to tell. I don't know enough about them myself to know if I agree or disagree with them. I guess they're so disciplined that they'd do anything they're told."

Lillian Collins, a white clerk who lived in San Leandro, was also willing to talk. In fact, she was so eager to share her impressions of the trial it was barely necessary to ask her questions. She told me she'd been wondering when the press would call. "The DA had a lousy case," she said. "Ramsey convicted himself. He told too many lies. The rebuttal witness, the janitor, D'Arcy, convinced me."

She said the vote was split ten to two, with two of the three blacks forming the minority. "It was a racial split all the way. They were intimidated. It wasn't a reasonable stance. There's no question but that Ramsey helped pistolwhip the tailor. All of us felt that way immediately, except the two black holdouts. We didn't believe that Ramsey asked Billings about going to the hospital."

"What about the fight at the Stanford Lounge?" I asked.

"Oh, there were certain people who went for the lesser assault charge. They attempted to malign the policemen. They couldn't find that Ramsey went for the gun because it was too dark to see."

"Was it the same people?"

"Sure it was. The split was the same all the way through. I don't think they knew what they were doing on the other charges or they wouldn't have voted to convict Ramsey of anything." She stopped. I could hear her taking a drag on a cigarette.

"You know, after the trial the bailiff told us if there were any threats to be sure to notify the court," she continued.

"Were there?"

"No. I don't think there were. But, well, I used to be more liberal. I don't like what's happened to me, you know. But, you know, at work someone got mugged in the parking lot in broad daylight. We've got security all over the place."

"Was it tense being on the jury?"

"Oh, no. I wasn't tense at all. It was an excellent jury. We worked quietly, methodically. The foreman made us all wait for our turn to speak. There weren't any arguments. The judge was great. He had everything in hand. I felt relaxed. I was confident."

My last call was to a black juror who had voted with the minority and who didn't want to discuss the trial. "It was my first jury duty," the juror told me. "I hope it's my last."

5

The Records Room

"All right. In the Willie Monroe matter, it is the order of the Court that by reason of the Defendant being in violation of his probationary conditions made by the Court that he be imprisoned in the State Penitentiary of the State of California for the term prescribed by law . . ."

Light spilled out of fixtures hanging from the ceiling on long gray rods. It splashed onto green metal cabinets, collecting in large pools. It settled onto the page of the transcript I was reading. Words blurred.

"*Adjustment on Probation*: Unsatisfactory. Defendant has missed numerous appointments, been late for others, canceled others, usually giving no or weak excuses. Defendant's only reported employment was with a painting contractor for two days. Defendant has made no payments in restitution to victim; balance remains at $22.00."

"If I'd known about probation, I'd never have agreed to it." I recalled what Mrs. Monroe had said. I was at a table in the records room, reading through Willie's file. Behind me were rows of files on huge long shelves. I wondered how many held stories like Willie's.

It was three years after Willie had pleaded guilty to robbery, three years after his trial. I'd thought about him often and how everyone had assumed he was guilty and marked him as a criminal from the beginning. A lawyer was next to me at the reading table. I wanted to ask him about the probation report. I wanted to ask what good sending Willie to prison would do now—wouldn't he come out trained for big-time crime? But the lawyer was reading. He was mouthing words. Ringing telephones, clacking typewriters, chattering voices all around me blended into a strange and hypnotic hum.

Maybe I'd ask a prosecutor I'd once interviewed. "Why would someone be sent to prison for missing appointments, for being unemployed, for refusing to pay back money he denied stealing?" I'd say.

"He was sent to prison for violating probation," I knew the prosecutor would tell me. "Read on."

I scanned the page. Willie had been arrested for drunken driving, for driving under the influence of drugs. He'd smashed up someone's car. Those weren't prison crimes, but he'd originally been convicted of a felony and then been spared prison on the understanding he would behave. The judge had told him prison would be the price for violating that understanding. It seemed a heavy price to pay.

"You have to remember that the guy did something crappy to someone else," I recalled the prosecutor saying. He'd been in a tiny plexiglass cell, and I'd asked him and his two officemates to tell me about their work and how they viewed the justice system. They'd been eager to talk and terribly earnest.

"We're the people's attorneys. We represent them when something wrong has been done to them as a whole," one prosecutor said.

"You have to look at the crime more than the criminal," said another.

"I never get to know the defendants. Any person can evoke sympathy and then you lose sight of what they did," said the third.

Looking down at Willie's folder, I wondered if he *had* done something, and if he had, what it was, and was he really responsible when the world was so reluctant to open up to him. I didn't see how I'd ever know when everyone was determined to keep him a stranger. A clerk brushed past me. I read some more.

Willie's probation had been revoked the year before too, after he'd been convicted of drunken driving and had failed to pay the fine. The judge sent him back to county jail for 90 days telling him that when he got out, he'd have to submit to a police search at any time, day or night, whether or not the policeman had a search warrant.

When the judge first sentenced Willie, right after his trial, he scolded him for having a probation report which said he showed no remorse for his crime. It didn't seem to occur to the judge that Willie might not think he was guilty.

"But the system operates on a presumption of guilt." I could hear the prosecutor's words. "The police and the DA's office screen out the innocent before they are ever charged. The business of the courts is to dispose of criminals. The prosecutor kind of controls the system by seeing where there are courtrooms free and then by deciding whether to charge a crime as a felony or as a misdemeanor, whether to send the defendant to superior or municipal court. If the prosecutor's charging policy is good, cases will get to the court on time and the system will work. The job of the DA's office is to keep the system unclogged."

"But if everyone presumes the defendant is guilty, what's the point of a trial?" I had asked.

"The trial is a symbolic procedure. Justice doesn't come out of criminal justice. We're just a piece of the system," the prosecutor replied.

"You have to understand that the purpose of the criminal justice system is to be a deterrent," his officemate added.

"Yes, punishment is the only way to prevent crime," the other officemate said.

"And sentencing is a compromise between punishment and rehabilitation," said the prosecutor.

I'd gone once with Willie's mother to visit Willie in county jail. He'd smiled out from behind a long row of tables where he sat with dozens of other prisoners. Afterwards, Mrs. Monroe had told me she was planning to have him stay with relatives in the valley during his probationary period, in the valley, far away from Oakland. She'd hoped he'd go back to school and learn to be a carpenter like his older brother. I imagined her face when she heard the judge sentence Willie to prison, the look of utter despair. I could see Willie nodding passively. I could see other prisoners waiting in line to be sentenced after him, as if they were at a graduation ceremony, as if they were going from high school to college.

"Justice doesn't come out of criminal justice," the prosecutor had said, and I had wondered what does. Does a deterrent come out of criminal justice? Do ways to keep the system unclogged? Those were probably answers, but there was something else too that I could feel but that I hadn't held long enough to know.

Near the reading table a clerk sorted out papers, using a huge slotted wheel. She inserted a paper into a slot and turned the wheel. She inserted another paper and turned the wheel again. I closed Willie's folder, placed it in the return box and left.

Part II: The Gamecourt

6

The People v. Lorenzo Johnny Smith

Would he plead or would he insist on going to trial?

The East Oakland robbery was a dead case. There was no doubt about it. They'd all but caught him at the bar stuffing his pockets with money. There didn't seem to be much point to a trial unless he simply wanted to put up one last fight before going behind the wall.

But the second charge was slippery. The Hayward robbery. The robber had gotten away, and the bartender hadn't been able to make his identification until after the police had hypnotized him, which raised all sorts of questions and doubts. Maybe a jury *would* acquit on the second charge. There was bargaining room.

The defender had just arrived in the courtroom, a short man taking short quick steps toward the judge's office, banging his fist on the bailiff's desk along the way, nodding coolly at his client. No sooner had he said, "Hello, judge," than the laughter began, loud laughter and talking. The door to the judge's office was open, and you could hear the defender's voice, and the judge's, and a third which must have been the prosecutor's.

Smith waited in a chair near the prisoners' door. He rubbed his eyes with his fingers. He had blue eyes. He pulled his pony tail, straight brown hair to the middle of his back. He looked at the

ceiling. He chewed his thumb. He cracked his knuckles. He looked
down at the floor and then he looked over at the doorway to the
judge's office. He was thirty-two, but he still had a babydoll face,
and he seemed small in the baggy white jumpsuit. His skin was pasty
white.

The bailiff was at the door to the judge's office. He wagged his
finger and Smith went inside, leaving the bailiff to stand at the
threshold, half in and half out, so he could watch two prisoners at
once — Smith and a woman in blue slacks and a blue county-jail
T-shirt who was sitting in the jury box. The woman was talking to a
man in the spectators' section. "Don't cook the broccoli too long.
It'll get mushy," she said, and the man said something back to her
which I couldn't hear.

It was quieter then. Except for an occasional word drifting out of
the judge's office, dissolving in the bailiff's cigarette smoke, you
couldn't hear what was going on. "Credit," someone said. I thought
it was the defender. Maybe they were offering Smith credit for the
year he'd already spent in jail waiting for the defender to go all the
way up to the court of appeals trying to get the Hayward charge
dropped. Maybe they were saying, you plead guilty, and you won't
have to serve that year. But that wouldn't be much of a deal. "Hayward or Oakland," someone else said. Were they offering to drop
one robbery charge if he pleaded to the other? I imagined Smith
resisting that offer too. I imagined him narrowing his eyes (I could
see the lines running down to the bridge of his nose) and saying,
"Man, that's no deal. You just hit me with that Hayward charge so
you'd have something to give away now."

Drop the gun charge too. Maybe that's what Smith was demanding. He was charged with armed robbery. The East Oakland robber
and the Hayward robber both used guns, and using a gun was a
heavy charge carrying a mandatory prison term. So maybe Smith
was asking for that, but then would there be enough left for the DA?
The DA had to feel he was getting a good deal too.

Maybe Smith wasn't demanding anything. I realized it was possible that he was being docile and letting his lawyer do the talking.
I'd imagined him as an active player, probably because of his age,
and because he had a long record. I was sure he'd plea bargained
before. But it was possible his lawyer and the DA had already
reached an agreement, and Smith was being silent, and it was the

judge who was balking. Someone had to be objecting to something. It was taking too much time.

The trouble with watching a plea bargaining was that almost everything except the final resolution went on behind closed doors — the offers, the counteroffers, the maneuvering. It was like seeing the checkmate, but not the plays leading up to it.

Except for the woman in the jury box and her husband in the spectators' section, I was the only one in the courtroom. Even the clerk was away from her desk. I hadn't been to the courthouse for several months, and as soon as I'd stepped inside the door I'd been aware of a strange light feeling, a feeling of belonging. In the elevator I ran into two lawyers I knew, and we exchanged gossip. Outside the courtroom one told me about an exciting trial. Inside everything looked less cluttered than I remembered. The room seemed bigger and airier. The people looked sportier, less businesslike than they had before. I felt different too — excited, eager for action. Recalling how depressed and confused the earlier trials had left me, I had the sense that I was closer to understanding what they were really about.

The defender came out into the courtroom to ask the clerk to call down to calendar court and tell the public defender he'd be late. "He'll know who my client is. I can't remember the name." The defender went back into the judge's office.

The prosecutor came out of the judge's office and lit up a cigarette. He was in shirt sleeves, and he lifted his jacket off a chair near the clerk's desk and put it on. Smith walked in next. He sat by the prisoners' door, rubbed his eyes with his fingers, then cracked his knuckles. I could hear the defender arguing with the judge.

The prosecutor told Smith, "You know, you're being stupid insisting on going to trial. You'll go down on the East Oakland one, no doubt about it. And there's a good chance the jury'll get you on the Hayward one too. You're stupider than I thought, Smith. You're thumbing your nose at the best deal you'll ever have."

"Lookit, man, I'm not trying to give you a hard time. Really. I just need more time to think about it." Wrinkles cut into Smith's forehead.

"You know, Pete's right," the defender broke in. He'd just come out of the judge's office and was adjusting his tie. "No jury's going to acquit you. Where there are two charges like this, juries compromise."

"Yeah, yeah. I know. I don't mean to give you a hard time, but, man, I haven't slept in three days. Lookit, the trial isn't until Tuesday. I'll decide by then."

"Hey!" The prosecutor was red-faced. "I'm not giving you that option! You decide today! Quit pushing me against the wall!"

"I'm not pushing you, man. I just need more time."

"What do you want me to do? Get the judge to waive time until next month when you're through in Contra Costa?" the defender asked Smith. He'd told me earlier Smith had another robbery charge against him in the neighboring county.

"Yeah," Smith replied. Maybe he figured that if he were convicted in Contra Costa he wouldn't have anything to lose by holding out for a trial in Oakland. I thought Smith was buying time. That was his game.

"Okay. We'll do it your way." The defender shook his head and stepped over to the lawyers' table and began talking to the judge who was now at his desk. "My client would like to waive time, your honor, until after his pretrial in Contra Costa."

The judge mumbled his agreement, the bailiff unlocked the prisoners' door, and Smith glowered at the prosecutor. "I don't trust you, mister. You got me screwed upstairs in jail."

When the bargaining resumed a month later, Smith was smiling. The charges against him in Contra Costa had been dismissed, and he looked like he was three inches taller. He was in the chair by the prisoners' door, beside the defender who was reading a xeroxed document. He looked over the defender's shoulder, pointed to something the document said and started laughing.

The judge was at his desk conducting court. He was asking a woman if she was satisfied with the proposed divorce settlement, and when she said yes, he droned out the words needed to dissolve the marriage.

The defender asked the clerk how much credit Smith would get for the time he'd already spent in jail. The clerk got out a sheet of paper and started figuring. The bailiff tacked a calendar on the wall. The judge got up and went into his office.

The defender asked the clerk how much credit Smith would get for the time he'd already spent in jail. The clerk got out a sheet of paper and started figuring. The bailiff tacked a calendar on the wall. The judge got up and went into his office.

"Which do you want to plead to, Hayward?" asked the prosecutor who'd just come into the courtroom.

"But he denies the Hayward robbery," the defender said.

"I deny both," Smith interrupted.

"George says if he pleads to Hayward, he'll get four years with credit for time served," the prosecutor insisted. (George was the judge.)

The three men huddled together, and the room was quiet. A reporter came down the aisle to ask the bailiff about a murder trial she was supposed to cover. It was scheduled for ten o'clock. The bailiff told her they were still selecting the jury. The reporter left, and the judge came out of his office.

Smith and the defender stood behind the lawyers' table, facing the judge. It was going to be official. I realized that there must have been negotiations during the previous month, and now the bargain was about to be sealed. How different this plea bargaining seemed from the trials I'd seen. It was a game.

"As I understand it, he's pleading to robbery only," said the judge. "All gun charges are dismissed, and he gets credit for time served plus one half for work time."

"I've got 526 days, so I'll get 200 some odd for work time," Smith said, joining the discussion.

"Contra Costa dismissed the charges against Mr. Smith, but he still has something pending in Santa Clara County," the defender told the judge.

"So I'll hold off the sentencing until that's resolved."

"Fine," the defender said. The judge began mumbling the terms of the agreement for the record.

"Wait a minute," Smith interrupted the judge. "Which charge am I pleading to?"

"The Oakland one, isn't it?" the judge replied.

"No." The defender shook his head, and he and the prosecutor stepped up to the judge's desk for a brief conference.

"Yes, it's Hayward," the judge announced when they were through.

The clerk read out the charge against Smith. "How do you plead?"

"Guilty," Smith said.

"Mr. Smith denies he committed this robbery," the defender said. "I told him it's the policy of the public defender's office not to have anyone plead unless they're guilty, but he's ignoring the policy of my office."

"That's because he's smarter than your office," the judge replied.

The bailiff unlocked the prisoners' door and motioned to Smith. As Smith turned to leave, the prosecutor stepped up to him and shook his hand.

7

The People v. Franklin Delano Butler

All around there was murmuring and muffled laughter. Behind me, a man whispered about last night's ball game. Across the aisle, a woman joked as she tugged off a plastic raincoat. Beside her, a man doing the daily crossword jogged his knee up and down. That made a rustling sound. There was a lot of rustling.

The man beside me was tapping his thumbs together and moving his lips to a marching beat. "You some kind of student or something?" he whispered loudly as I opened up my notebook and started taking notes.

"A reporter," I whispered back, taking stock of the worn suit and the mess of fine gray hair. I explained that I was planning to write a story about an everyday trial.

"This is the third time I've been called up for jury duty," he told me. "I never get chosen. It's like a lottery. Who knows, maybe this'll be my lucky day." His green eyes twinkled from behind rimless glasses.

Suddenly the spectators' section was quiet. There were a few coughs, and then it was still. It was as if someone had sent out a secret signal. "You are here to partake in the selection of a jury in the case of the people of the state of California versus Franklin Delano Butler," the judge boomed out. He rested his plump arms on the

desk and he studied the panel: twelve in the jury box, twenty-two in
the audience. "Butler is accused of a felony, to wit, armed robbery.
This allegation is simply a charge, it isn't evidence. Paramount to
our system of justice is a presumption of innocence." Everyone's
eyes were on the judge. Everyone was straining to hear his every
word. His round face glowed.

"Does anyone know the defendant?" the judge asked, looking
toward the jury box. "Is there any reason why anyone can't be fair?"
Twelve heads bobbed from side to side. "Jurors must be free from
prejudice and sympathy," the judge cautioned. "The feeling of any
emotional response is unacceptable," he said.

"Now, has anyone ever been the victim of a crime?" he asked,
pushing back his chair so he was arm's length from his desk and
almost touching the American flag. Mr. Blanchard in seat number
three raised his hand to say he was once stabbed. The judge reminded everyone that Butler wasn't on trial for that. Everyone
nodded and glanced at Butler who was beside his lawyer at the
lawyers' table—processed hair combed back from a thin brown
boyish face.

"Does it bother you to be a trier of the truth?" The spotlight was
off the judge and on the prosecutor who was standing by the jury
box, pulling on the lapels of his tailored tweed jacket which flared at
the bottom, emphasizing the curve to his back and shoulders.

"No," Peter Sullivan, the longhaired young man in seat number
one, replied. Sullivan was holding the microphone the bailiff had
handed him close to his lips, and he told the prosecutor he lived in
Berkeley and used to sell ceramics on Telegraph Avenue near the
university.

"Can you think of any reason why you can't be fair?" the prosecutor asked.

"No," Sullivan replied.

"Will sympathy get in your way?"

Sullivan thought for a moment. "No, sympathy works two
ways—for the victim and for the defendant," he said.

"Do you think that seeing the defendant throughout the trial and
not the victim will make you have more sympathy for the defendant?"

"No." Sullivan shook his head.

"Can you say to yourself sympathy has nothing to do with this
case?"

"Yes."

"If I have just one witness will that bother you?"

"No."

"If the defense has more witnesses than I do, does that mean his case is stronger?"

"No."

"What if I put on just one witness who identifies the defendant, an ID witness, and no circumstantial evidence, no fingerprints, et cetera, will you give my case weight?"

"Yes," Sullivan mumbled.

"Can you dismiss all feelings of sympathy?"

"I already answered that," Sullivan wailed.

"Yeah, let's get going!" a plump woman in a brown polkadot dress squealed from the audience.

The prosecutor's face reddened, and he began questioning the man in seat number two.

"Jesus, him too. What do they expect us to do, castrate our emotions or something?" The man to my left grinned all the way past the gold tooth in the side of his jaw, first at me and then at the woman on his other side. Everyone was whispering and shifting around in their chairs, and the noise never entirely subsided, not even later when the defender, a tall man, stood primly behind his chair to begin his list of questions which was also very long.

The lawyers didn't actually choose the jury until the next morning when the prosecutor bowed and thanked and dismissed Arthur Hodgkins, a young unemployed black man who walked quickly to the clerk's desk, where he received a written dismissal, and then down the aisle and out the door. As the clerk dipped into the wooden container for a slip of paper with a name, everyone craned their necks, and then everyone looked around when Cranston Dickey was called and a stout white man hurried to the jury box and Hodgkins' seat, number nine.

After Dickey was finished answering questions, the challenge was with the defender, but the defender remained seated and announced he was passing.

The judge frowned, and so did the prosecutor, and the prosecutor stood to thank and excuse Sarah Tillingham, a young black clerk who tossed back her head as she marched to the clerk's desk and then out of the room.

"He's getting rid of all the blacks. Write that down!" the man beside me whispered hoarsely, at the same time waving me still because it was the defender's turn again, and again the defender was passing.

The prosecutor excused a young unemployed black woman.

The defender passed.

"Why doesn't the defender bump that old guy, the army officer? He'll be proprosecution for sure," the man beside me whispered.

The army officer certainly hadn't sounded like he would have much sympathy for any defendant. I didn't say that though. The man beside me might end up on the jury, and I wasn't sure what I could properly say, so I shrugged my shoulders and told him I didn't know.

The prosecutor excused a white woman who said it might bother her to vote to send someone to jail.

The defender passed again.

"Why doesn't he excuse that lady whose uncle is a cop?" the man beside me poked me with his elbow.

"Well, *she's* not a cop," the woman on his left answered.

"Nah, doesn't matter. He's crazy if you ask me."

I looked around the spectators' section at the remaining panelists and thought to myself that maybe he didn't think the people who were left would be very different.

"Maybe he's trying to embarrass the prosecutor. Get him to leave at least one black on the jury, you know?" the man said, and I grinned because just then the prosecutor hunched up his shoulders the way people do when they feel conspicuous. "Will you be prejudiced against me for excusing so many people?" he asked a panelist.

Jury selection ended. One black, an accountant from Oakland, remained.

The unchosen jury panelists funneled out of the courtroom, leaving only two women and a small girl in the spectators' section, and me. One of the women was wearing an ankle length dress and a lacy shawl, and her hair went straight along her thin brown face, and then it flared out in a semicircle at her shoulders. She was in the first row with the child in her lap, next to her companion, directly behind the defendant.

The clerk swore the jury in, and the prosecutor delivered his opening argument. Then we recessed for lunch and reconvened a little after two, which was when Clifford Rossi took the stand. Rossi was the victim, the man who'd been robbed nine months before. He was a square man with big shoulders; he seemed at ease on the stand. He told the jury he was the owner of the Orange Blossom Nightclub in downtown Oakland. He said that at the time of the robbery he'd been alone washing glasses behind the bar. It had been seven thirty in the evening. Two black men had come into the club, one of them wearing a hat and dark glasses. They'd looked around and had left almost immediately because the band hadn't yet arrived. Rossi said the robber came in maybe ten minutes later, pointing a gun, calling Rossi by name, saying he wanted Rossi's money. Rossi said he thought he must know the man because the man had known his name. Thinking it was all a joke, he started laughing. But then he stopped laughing.

Rossi's story was a variation on a theme I was coming to know well. Watching him there on the stand looking straight at the jury, I thought he was a polished version of Jeremy Tyson or Mrs. Drummond.

Rossi must have testified for an hour. I listened carefully to what he said and took copious notes. After a while I realized that despite his polish, my attention had shifted from him to the lawyer. In the beginning the prosecutor was as stiff as a solider. Rossi, with his forthright answers, was clearly the star. But then the prosecutor relaxed. He loosened up. He got Rossi to say just the right things. He took control.

He got Rossi to say there hadn't been any problem seeing the robber's face because there were 150, 25-watt bulbs around the dance floor and more bulbs along the bar. He got Rossi to tell the jury that he'd had a chance to look at the robber's face when he was moving out from behind the bar, again when he was walking to his office, again when he was opening the safe, and again when the robber was tying him up. He got Rossi to say that each look at the robber had been very long, that he (Rossi) had stalled for time because the band was overdue. He got Rossi to say that he'd taken as long to open the safe as he thought he could without alarming the robber. The prosecutor got Rossi to say he was a bartender by profession. It was his job to remember faces. As the prosecutor moved from one question to the next, as he scored point after point, his expression softened, his eyes began to shine. By the time he was through, he was prancing back and forth in front of the jury.

On the other hand, during cross examination the defender was as prim as a choir boy, and he never broke the pose. His tone was so even, so consistent, you couldn't tell which questions were important. He began with what I assumed were routine questions — who owns the nightclub, who works there, things like that. Then he asked a few questions about the money that was stolen. Apparently Rossi told the police he thought the robber stole $2,500, but later he said he discovered his loss was $7,500, and there were questions about that. There were questions about where Rossi had his car keys too, and about the two men who came into the club before the robber, and then the inevitable questions about all of the inconsistencies between what Rossi was saying in court and what he'd originally told the police. The defender's questions flowed one into the next, which seemed to throw Rossi off balance and put the defender in control. I had no idea where the defender was heading, but it occurred to me that creating just that mystery was probably one of his plays.

By 3:45 the lawyers were through. Rossi had left. Two policemen had testified, making it official that Rossi had reported the robbery and that he'd identified Butler as the robber from a mug shot. After the judge adjourned for the day, I picked up my belongings and made ready to leave. The two women and the child were still in the front row. They seemed to belong with the defendant. The courtroom was so quiet I could hear the court reporter folding up her paper tape. I could hear the air blowing in from the register near the ceiling. I missed the noise and the excitement of the morning. I missed the people.

Waiting for the elevator, I felt someone tapping me on the shoulder. I turned around, and there was the man from jury selection. "Hey there!" It was good seeing him. He told me he'd been excused from jury duty. He said he was a free man. He said he'd taken the afternoon off and had spent it watching the murder trial across the hall.

"So what's happening with the robbery?" he asked me. "Does the prosecutor have any kind of case? How did the guy get robbed?" His eyes were wide open, begging me to answer his questions.

I told him quickly how Rossi got robbed, and I told him I thought Rossi made a good witness, and I told him what a good job I thought the prosecutor did. It was a relief to be able to express my opinions at last to this man who was no longer a prospective juror.

"So the prosecutor did a good job," my friend interjected, "but does he have a case?"

"Well, he pulled a little here, and he stretched a little there." I demonstrated with my hands.

"In other words he played the little he had for all it was worth." My friend sized up the situation.

I laughed and agreed the case was pretty slim. It was just as he'd described it during *voir dire*: no fingerprints, no gun, no supporting evidence, just Rossi's identification. I told my friend more about Rossi's testimony and about the points I thought the prosecutor had scored. I moved as quickly as I could because what I really wanted to talk to him about was cross examination and the defender's strategy. "I'm not sure what the defender's driving at," I finally got a chance to say. "I couldn't tell which of his questions were important."

"That's obviously his strategy," my friend shrugged. "Confuse the witness. Lull him to sleep with boring questions and then, powee!"—he whacked his thigh—"trap him into saying something awful!"

I was sure he was right. I recalled that by the end of cross examination the prosecutor had begun hunching up his shoulders again, the way he had during *voir dire*, but I couldn't see what point the defender had scored. "What did Rossi say that was so awful?" I asked.

"Well, it's not the inconsistencies between what he told the police and what he said later. That's too obvious. Anyway, they all find inconsistencies. They learn how to do that in law school. They all read Bailey. He's the expert. I know because my nephew's a lawyer."

I nodded.

"So it must be something else." He was stroking his chin, making me feel like Watson waiting for one of Sherlock Holmes' pronouncements. "The guy wasn't really robbed! He wasn't robbed! He's making the whole thing up to collect insurance!" In his excitement my friend was shouting, and several people turned around to stare at him. We'd come out of the elevator, and we were in the ground floor hallway.

"Great." I was giggling. "The only problem with your theory is that the prosecutor asked Rossi if he was insured, and Rossi said he wasn't."

"He wasn't insured? Jesus. He must be a jerk. I'll bet he is now."
My friend winked. He stroked his chin some more. I waited. Finally, "The man who came in before the robber! Of course. How stupid. The one with the dark glasses and the hat!" my friend cried.

"Yes, I'll bet *he's* the real robber!"

"Sure he is! Mark my words. The defender's going to prove it!"

"I think you're right." It was so obvious I felt a little dumb for not having thought of it myself. "You know, the defender brought out that Rossi told the police the robber was wearing a hat, although Rossi denied he'd ever said that."

"Of course he denied it. He knew where the defender was heading. My good woman, I predict," my friend took a deep bow, "tomorrow the defender is going to electrify the courtroom with startling proof that the man in the hat is none other than the robber."

We were both laughing. We were outside by then, and the sun was shining gloriously. My friend said he'd try to get back to the courthouse the next day. "I'll take off from work. Gotta find out how this ends," he said, and he shook my hand.

It was a little before ten. The jury was still upstairs, and the two lawyers and the judge were in the judge's office, and Butler was at the lawyers' table, his back to the spectators' section. I could see him moving his finger on the glassy surface of the table, tracing and retracing a figure eight.

"He cross examined his own witness?" the bailiff cried out. He was at his desk, talking on the phone.

Butler turned to look at the bailiff. He was grinning.

It was strange seeing him smile. I think it was the second time I'd seen his face.

The two women and the girl came into the courtroom, the one in the long dress holding the child by the hand. They took their seats in the front row, directly behind Butler. Butler turned his chair around after the bailiff said it was okay to talk but not to touch. The women pressed up against the railing, full of smiles, while Butler, with a devilish grin, teased the girl. Then the smiles were gone and Butler was talking, saying something, I couldn't hear it all, about being framed.

* * *

The trial didn't resume until the afternoon because there'd been some mixup in serving Officer Vincent Graves a subpoena. Graves was supposed to be the first witness for the defense, and the lawyers were on the phone most of the morning trying to track him down. They finally reached his wife and left a message. The judge was hopping mad. He said he'd wait until after lunch, no longer. The courts were too busy for such delays. "You're both young. You'll learn from experience," he told the lawyers. He was yelling.

After lunch the officer still hadn't shown, and the judge backed down and gave the defender ten more minutes. But Officer Graves still didn't arrive, so the judge had the bailiff press the buzzer near his desk to signal the jury to come down. Just as the jurors were filing in through the side door, Officer Graves hurried into the courtroom out of breath, wearing a light sports suit, looking rather like one of the mod squad cops on TV. He couldn't have testified for longer than five minutes, just long enough to make it official that some of what Rossi had told the police was different from what he'd said on the stand. He'd said his loss was only $2,500, for example; he'd said the robber was wearing a hat.

A woman named Monica Peterson was supposed to testify next, but she was late too. When the defender asked the judge for another recess to give him time to find her, the judge glared at him, and the defender called Butler to the stand. Since the defender had told me before the trial that he had only three witnesses, I was sure that Monica Peterson's testimony would be key. I was sure the defender wasn't going to be able to make his case without her, although he certainly didn't look worried.

Butler stepped slowly up to the clerk's desk to be sworn in. Then he stepped slowly to the stand. Once he was seated, he smoothed out the wrinkles in the plaid suit he was wearing, and he pulled up the collar of his flowered shirt, and he brushed the dust off his shiny platform shoes. He glanced at the microphone. He stared at the defender. He seemed shy. Shy, or he was acting.

I was sorry my friend from jury selection hadn't shown up. I was confused by the defense, and I would have valued his ideas. It seemed to me that if Butler turned out to be the only other defense witness, our theory couldn't be right. At least I couldn't imagine how Butler alone could finger someone else as the real robber. Maybe it was going to be like Jonah Kay's trial. Maybe Butler would come up with an alibi. Maybe he'd been in Honolulu the previous August. Maybe he had an airline ticket to prove it. Maybe he'd been in jail. The defender looked confident. The prosecutor didn't.

"Mr. Butler, can you tell the jury when it was you were arrested?" the defender began.

"In the middle of November. Six months ago."

"I see. Now, where were you living at the end of last summer, at the end of last August?" the defender asked.

"I was living with Monica Peterson. She's a friend of my mother's. I lived with her for a month, and then I moved in the middle of September to live with my sister."

"During that period did you ever have a lot of money or a gun?"

"No, I didn't." Butler was talking softly. He was practically whispering.

"When was it you said you left Mrs. Peterson's residence?"

"I left sometime in September, the end of September."

"And why did you leave?"

"I left because she had three kids, and I had been there a while. I wasn't working, so I wasn't able to contribute anything to the family and I felt I should leave."

The defender asked Butler how old he was and how tall he was. Butler replied that he was twenty-two and five feet nine and a half in his bare feet — a few years younger and a couple of inches taller than Rossi had said the robber was. Butler said the summer before he'd worn a Lord Jesus hair style, straight and close to his head. (Rossi had said the robber's hair was sticking straight out.)

"Do you remember where you were the night of August 27th, Mr. Butler?" the defender asked.

"No, sir. I can't remember where I was. I wasn't arrested until three months after that. I have tried to remember where I was. I have tried very much."

"Mr. Butler, did you rob Clifford Rossi or the Orange Blossom Nightclub?"

"No, sir."

"Have you ever been to the Orange Blossom?"

"Yes, sir. I was there twice. It was last spring. They had Billy Johnstone." Butler looked at the jury for the first time. "He's a jazz musician. I'm a big fan of his," he said, smiling.

The defender announced that he was through, and he sat down.

There was no alibi, no airplane ticket, but he didn't seem nervous, and on cross examination the prosecutor did. The prosecutor only asked one or two questions, going so quickly I didn't have time to write them down.

As Butler returned to his seat, I noticed him looking to the back of the courtroom. The woman in the long dress had just come in. She'd been gone since mid morning. She nodded her head and the defender followed her out of the courtroom, returning a minute later with a tall, dark-skinned woman who told the clerk her name was Monica Peterson. She was attractive, probably in her forties. It seemed to me more likely now that she was going to supply Butler with an alibi than finger someone else as the robber.

The defender asked Peterson if Butler had lived with her the previous summer.

She replied that he had. She said she couldn't remember exactly for how long, probably six weeks, from the end of July to the beginning of September. She said he moved out just before school started.

"And was Mr. Butler employed at the time?" the defender asked her.

"No, he wasn't. He'd been trying for a job at the shipyards, but they were having a layoff. That's why I offered to have him stay with me because he didn't have any place else to go."

"Now, Mrs. Peterson, did you ever see Mr. Butler with a gun?"

"No, I haven't."

"Did you ever see him with a lot of money?"

"No. He took my little boy shopping and bought him some candy and soda, and that's the most money I saw him with. I've had to buy his cigarettes." Peterson said he finally moved out because he couldn't pay his way.

Peterson didn't say a thing about the Orange Blossom Nightclub or anyone else who might have been the robber or where Butler had been on the night of the robbery. Her testimony concerned a quiet young man who had been unemployed and who therefore had a perfectly good motive for robbery.

I tiptoed into the courtroom where they were holding the murder trial and stood in the back and looked around at the dozen or so people in the audience (murder trials always draw audiences), but my friend from jury selection wasn't there.

Out in the hallway, I smiled at the woman in the long dress. She told me her name was Cheryl; she said she was Franklin's sister, and after Monica was through making a phone call, they were going upstairs to visit Franklin in the courthouse jail.

"He's been in jail the whole time?" I asked her.

She nodded. "Six months. That's a long time when they have so little evidence. Rossi's word. That's all they have. How's the jury to know if he's lying?"

I told her I agreed. Rossi didn't even have to be lying. He could be mistaken. The prosecutor was asking the jury to guess whether he was right. That was no basis for sending someone to prison.

"Rossi identified Franklin because someone told him he did it. He's going on rumor," she said.

"Why didn't the defender bring that out?" I asked.

"Oh, he said it'd do Franklin more harm than good. That's what he said, but you know those public defenders." She looked over her shoulder. Monica was coming out of the phone booth. "The reason Monica was late was because she was afraid to come and testify," Cheryl told me. "She was afraid they might put her in jail." Cheryl pulled her shawl tightly about her shoulders. "Black people are afraid of the courts."

"That's the truth." It was Monica. She was standing beside me, buttoning up her coat. "They've got all our men in jail," she said.

I had trouble listening to the prosecutor's closing argument. I'd expected more than a routine ID witness case. I felt let down. I watched the prosecutor standing stiffly behind the metal lectern, referring to notes, and then I studied the judge whose eyes were half closed and whose head was nodding. The judge hadn't had much to do during the trial, there hadn't been any real disputes between the two lawyers. He hadn't been called on to referee. He'd been more of a time keeper. I stared at the shiny wooden railing, and I studied the jurors' faces too, and every now and then one of the prosecutor's phrases caught my ear, and I jotted it down. "Use the law, the facts, and your god given common sense," for example. And: "The bartender didn't care how much money he lost. He was interested in catching the thief." And: "You've seen how reliable Officer Graves is. He's the one who held us up all morning." And: "The defender will tell you my case is weak. That's because his job is to put the truth in the worst possible light." I watched the defender get to his feet and step out in front of the jury. I studied the jurors' faces some more as he told them that a judge I'd never heard of once said that more people were wrongly convicted on the basis of ID witness testimony than on any other kind of evidence.

It was 11:17 — I know because I'd just looked at the clock, and I'd written that down — when the defender's tone changed. He was saying he thought Rossi was mistaken in his identification, and then he said, "I think Rossi deliberately lied about the amount of money the robber took." The defender smiled, I made a note of that too, and then he talked quietly. He explained that he thought Rossi had lied because $7,500 makes a much better tax writeoff than $2,500. "The judge will tell you that a witness willfully false in one part of his testimony is to be mistrusted in the rest," the defender said. He was reciting the same legal instruction that had trapped John Ramsey, and probably Willie Monroe. The prosecutor's eyes were downcast, as if he'd expected this move all along. But the judge looked wide awake, and so did the clerk and the bailiff, and I'm sure I did too.

"Of course that's it! It wasn't ever the man in the hat. That was just a decoy!" I imagined my friend from jury selection would have said if he had been here. I realized that his first theory, that Rossi had lied about being robbed to collect insurance money, had been pretty close to the mark.

As the defender talked on, I thought how strange it was to hear him using the lying instruction. Other defenders had told me they'd like to see it abolished since it was so often used against defendants who had stretched a little here and rearranged a little there in their desperation to please the jury. I wondered if the defender had ever used that instruction to his advantage before. I felt like I was watching a tennis player playing his opponent's side of the net.

"Nah, it's done all the time," I could hear the ghost of my friend from jury selection say. "My nephew says when you go to law school you're trained to play both sides."

"So what do you think? Will the jury buy it? Will they turn on Rossi instead of Butler?"

"Ah, that is the question," the ghost of my friend replied, suddenly evaporating as the prosecutor got up to rebut the defender. Rossi didn't lie about the money, the prosecutor told the jury, but

even if he did, that had no bearing on the validity of his identification. "This trial should be called *Great Illusions*," he said, "because
all the defender has been able to do is raise an illusion of doubt."

As the prosecutor walked away from the lectern, the defender
jumped up to shake his hand.

"Jesus, look at that!" said the ghost of my friend.

"The black one, he'll acquit, and the hippie from Berkeley, and the
two Chicanos — the guy who used to be in the band and the one with
the beard who snickered when the DA excused the black woman
during *voir dire*." I was going down the list of jurors, and Cheryl was
looking over my shoulder as I ticked off names. The jury had been
out deliberating for over an hour, and the bailiff was away from his
desk, so it was just the clerk and the two of us in the courtroom.

"That woman who sat in the second row. The one with bleached
blonde hair? She'll want to convict, and so will the old guy, the CPA,
and the retired army man," I continued.

"We've all got to do our duty to god, you know. People can put
aside prejudice," Cheryl replied.

"You think they'll believe the defender?"

She smiled. She couldn't have been more than 25, but the way she
smiled and the way she had her shawl so tight around her shoulders,
made her look much older. "This is a microcosm of the outside," she
said. "People are afraid of each other. They think we wear our hair
funny. We used to straighten it, and now it's natural, and it may not
be good, but that's the way it is." She was twisted around in her
chair, facing me, her eyes boring into mine. "You know, I told my
little girl she was coming to court. Did she know what prison was? I
asked her. 'Yes,' she said, she knew. 'Well,' I told her, 'you have to
be very quiet in court to help Uncle Franklin stay out of prison.' She
has to learn early. I can't bear the whole burden myself. Girl, it's as
frightening looking at that child's eyes pointing at you asking why
things are this way as it is looking at a gun."

There was the sound of the courtroom doors swinging open. I
turned to see the defender and prosecutor coming in.

"No one here?"

"No," I called out, relieved to see them. I didn't want to think
about what Cheryl was saying. I slipped out of my chair and joined

them in the back of the courtroom. "What do you think?" I asked
eagerly.

"Acquittal," the defender shrugged.

"Acquittal? Really?" I looked at the prosecutor.

"Probably." He shrugged too.

I told them that surprised me, and I volunteered my theory about
who would be voting to convict, but neither lawyer seemed terribly
impressed. "If you're so sure of acquittal, why did you ever bring
this to trial?" I asked the prosecutor.

"Just because a case is hard to prove doesn't keep me from trying
it!" he shot back. He left.

"He seems terribly intent on winning," I told the defender. We
both laughed. I asked him what would happen to Franklin if he
wasn't acquitted, if the jury hung up instead. He told me Franklin
had another charge against him, auto theft. He said Franklin was
going to plead guilty to that. Auto theft, the defender explained,
could be charged either as a felony or as a misdemeanor. "The
prosecutor's waiting to see what happens here before he decides how
to charge it."

"I'm not following," I told him.

"It will be a misdemeanor if the jury acquits Butler of the robbery."

"But if they hang up, it will be a felony?"

"Exactly."

"That's why the prosecutor came to trial? The whole trial's been a
plea bargaining?" I asked in disbelief. "The jury's being asked to
spin a wheel, to decide Franklin's fate in a case they don't know
anything about?"

The defender laughed again, but I didn't think it was funny.

When I returned to my seat, the bailiff was coming in through the
prisoners' door, jangling a bunch of keys.

"You know, it's the little things that sometimes are important."
Cheryl took up as though I'd never been away. "Like that bailiff.
When it was recess, Franklin lit up a cigarette. He asked the bailiff
for an ashtray, and the bailiff said he didn't have one, but he did.
This is the first time I've been in the courts. All the defendants are
black." She tugged at her shawl. "Constitution. Bill of Rights. Girl,
we've been fed a bad truth. They tell us to go to school. Get an
education. Can't get a job without an education. So we get an educa-

tion and what happens? Nothing. That's what happens. You get
somewhere and they set up six more hoops for you to jump through.
Franklin finished Berkeley High, you know. He was planning to go
to community college. He picked up the forms and everything. But
now look where he is. I've introduced him into the black arts movement. He's an unskilled worker. What can you do with a high school
degree?" She sighed. "The DA and all the others, they don't care
about justice. The public defender's job is to defend and the DA's
job is to prove Franklin is guilty."

"I know," I said. I touched Cheryl's arm. I did know. It wasn't
the truth that mattered. This trial was like the others I'd seen. I'd
known all along, but I'd blocked the unpleasantness out of my mind
by playing games. I was sure the defender was doing the same. He
wasn't an insensitive man. The problem though was that if the trial
was a game, Franklin Butler was a pawn.

"Life, liberty and the pursuit of happiness. It's lies, girl, it's lies.
That's why there's the protest. They block us from developing ourselves and when someone commits a crime they wonder why. You
know what that jury's going to say? They're going to say he wasn't
working, he was laying up on his family, he must've done it." Cheryl
stroked the fringe of her shawl. "Upstairs it's all black men. I only
saw two whites. It looked like a bunch of caged-up black men.
That's fear, girl, caging all the black men up. That jury's full of
fear."

The jury hung up nine to three for acquittal. Some of the jurors
stayed on to tell the prosecutor all about it after everyone else had
left. They were down in the lobby, in a semicircle around the prosecutor: Mr. James, the black juror, who said he'd voted to acquit, and
Mrs. Blake and Mr. Lopez who said they'd been for conviction.

"What convinced you he was guilty?" the prosecutor asked Mr.
Lopez.

"He was so passive," Mr. Lopez said, gesturing with his hands.

"But blacks are often meek when confronted by authority," Mr.
James explained.

"Yes, but he *acted* guilty. He didn't remember anything."

"Yeah," Mrs. Blake agreed. "If he wasn't guilty, why didn't he
say more? I know I would have. Besides, usually on weekends
people know what they do."

Mr. James smiled and stepped back.

"What made you vote to acquit?" the prosecutor asked James.

"It was Rossi taking the money off the top. I had the feeling of Butler's guiltiness, but I had to go with the evidence, and the law says if someone is untrustworthy in one respect you have to discount the rest."

"But the issue isn't the money," Mrs. Blake interrupted. She was very excited. "Rossi had nothing to gain by identifying the wrong man."

Mr. Lopez's head bobbed rapidly up and down in agreement.

"And I knew Butler had a record, or else why would they have his mug shot," Mrs. Blake added.

"Right on. You know, the first vote was six to six, but then three changed. One guy said there are so many criminals loose out on the street anyway, what difference does it make if one more wiggles out of it," Mr. Lopez said.

"Yeah, I know. That's the trouble," the prosecutor said. "I had a real strong case. I really did, but I couldn't use the evidence. My hands were tied."

"Sure. All those judges," Mrs. Blake said sympathetically.

"What was the evidence?" Mr. Lopez asked eagerly.

"Well, for starters, what would the jury have done if it'd known Butler was a dope addict . . ."

"That's all we would have needed! A dope addict will rob his own mother," Mr. James said to me. He was putting on his coat, starting for the door.

"The jury would have convicted?" I asked him.

"Oh, sure. All the prosecutor needed was a hair more evidence. The defender did an excellent job, you realize. I've been on a debate team and I've argued both sides. The defender played his side to the hilt."

8

Nine O'Clock at the Elevators

"Hey there! I loved your stipulation!" Laughter echoed in the marble corridor. Two men shook hands.

"What're you up to now? What've you got there?" the first one asked, jabbing at a large plastic folder secured under his friend's right arm.

"Oh, it's real nice. Let me show you." The second man winked. He dropped the folder to the floor and opened it up to a cardboard chart with bright green and red lines.

"Just what you need to clinch the case. Good visuals!" Their laughter carried down to the ends of three hallways where men with briefcases were pulling open heavy doors and hurrying in to the elevators.

"Morning, judge."

"Hey, Bob. Hear you played a mean game of golf last Saturday."

"Pretty fair, judge, pretty fair."

"Howie's dropped the Neal case?"

"Oh, yeah. Took his wife to Hawaii."

"Oh, I hadn't heard. He didn't win the Butler case, you know."

The hallway was crowded. When an elevator came, everyone pushed to get on, but there wasn't enough room. A few sneaked onto a down elevator going to the basement; when the doors opened again after the elevator came back up, there they were, smiling victoriously.

Two men with TV cameras set firmly on their shoulders were standing to one side, chewing gum, waiting for a city official who was scheduled for trial. A man squatted on his heels, waiting too. A boy was next to him, cross legged on the floor.

A man wearing a vest underneath an unbuttoned jacket pushed up to the front of the crowd. "Hi, Jan." Beaming, he put his arm around a young woman in a pink skirt with red trim. "You look just like an ice cream cone!"

"An ice cream cone?" she giggled.

"An ice cream cone." He tweaked her cheek.

"He shot himself in the foot!" a uniformed bailiff was saying to two plainclothes listeners. "He tells the judge, 'My client can't make it because he shot himself in the foot!' " The listeners howled. "I says, 'Man, I'm baby sitting ten prisoners waiting to see the judge while you're making excuses. I'd better throw 'em some meat or I'll have a revolt on my hands!' " Side splitting laughter.

In the elevator everyone was sober, standing straight and tall so as not to touch.

9

The People v. Calvin Thompson

"Officer Cole, directing your attention to October 18th of this year, at approximately six o'clock p.m., did you have occasion to be at 1985, 65th Street in Berkeley?"

"Yes."

"For what reason?"

"Investigation of an occurrence of a dog bite. There was a dog which had bitten the person up the street. Mr. Thompson was being cited for having an unleashed and unlicensed dog."

The scene was a small windowless municipal courtroom on the second floor of a downtown Berkeley office building. The proceeding was a preliminary examination, a hearing to determine if the state had enough evidence against Calvin Thompson to bind him over to superior court for trial. Thompson had two heavy charges against him, two charges of felonious assault against a police officer, although knowing about the case it was hard to believe the judge would take it seriously. I was sure he would find a way to resolve it that day in the lower court.

The room was practically empty. Still the officer spoke as if to an audience, carefully enunciating the ends of words and sentences, bringing what he said to life with his hands. This and the sound-proofed ceiling bearing down on the carpeted floor exaggerated his tall muscular build and thrust him into the spotlight, leaving everyone else—the lawyers, the defendant and the judge—on the sidelines.

"How long were you on the scene before ascertaining that Calvin Thompson was the owner of the dog?"

"Probably about ten to fifteen minutes. The dog was in the Thompson residence when we first found it, and then Mr. Thompson let it run out the front door, and then," the officer smiled, "we were able to convince Mr. Thompson to assist us in restraining the dog." The officer glanced at the judge, his eyes and his smile conveying his meaning: Thompson had been uncooperative, disrespectful of authority. Had it been because he'd let his dog run loose when the officer wanted it kept inside? Or had Thompson said something to offend the officer? Perhaps it had simply been his manner. The officer didn't say. "The dog had to go for a ten-day quarantine," he continued his testimony, "and as soon as I had finished writing the citation, I went to my car and called the pound. After that I checked with our telecom center and found out there was a traffic warrant outstanding on Mr. Thompson."

The officer pulled the microphone closer to his mouth. "I went back to Thompson's house and I told him there was the warrant, illegally parking his car, and he said, 'I already paid it,' and he brushed past me and went down the steps." As the officer testified, the judge nodded his head. "I followed him. I said, 'No, you haven't paid, and you will have to be arrested,' but Thompson brushed me aside again and he said, 'I'm not going to jail.'" Taking Thompson's part, the officer made his voice gruffer.

"I caught up with him and grabbed onto his left arm," the officer went on, grabbing his own left arm, so convincingly that the muscles along Thompson's back twitched and quivered, as they must have that day before Thompson pulled free, before he continued on down the street carefully measuring his strides, hands at his thighs balled into fists, boyish black eyes shining against smooth ebony skin. A neighbor in a yellow house peeked out from behind sheer curtains, and two of Thompson's friends trailed Thompson and the officer, keeping a safe distance behind.

"I tried to grab his left arm again, but he just turned and pushed me in the chest with his right hand. Well, Officer Loehmann was also there. Officer Loehmann ran around and tried to grab ahold of

Thompson from the rear, but Thompson twisted free." Officer Cole made another go at Thompson, and Thompson broke away, and Officer Loehmann tried to grab Thompson all the way around in a strangle hold, and Thompson eluded him too. Then Officer Cole grabbed Thompson's arm, only to have to release his hold because Thompson's two friends were suddenly upon him, wrenching the billy club from his hand.

By then the neighbor was on her front porch, cupping a wrinkled hand to her ear, straining for words lost in the roar of the BART train two blocks away, and another neighbor was by his '65 green Chevy, watching an older buxom woman running from the back of the Thompson house.

"At that point I grabbed him, I believe it was around the head. Well, then he reached around with his hand and grabbed onto my left eye. I can't exactly show you how his arms were, but he had his hand, fingernails, in my eyes — like that." The officer was standing.

"Did you suffer any injuries at the time?"

"Yes, I suffered a scratch here, and one here, and one here, and one on my lip." The officer pivoted around on his right foot so that he was facing the judge.

"And what happened then?"

"Well, I couldn't remove his hand from my eye without letting go of him, so I held on. Eventually, I believe it was his mother who pulled his hand away."

Thompson's mother was in the courtroom when the judge announced that the state had presented enough evidence to bind Thompson over for trial in superior court on two counts of felonious assault against a police officer. Her features were like her son's, although her expression was less determined. Age had softened the lines. I looked at her, thinking how outraged I would have been to have my son charged as a felon for such an offense. But Mrs. Thompson didn't look outraged. She look like she expected what had happened.

When the defender dashed into the courtroom, wearing his gray suit like armor, carrying the bargain like an offering on a tray, he motioned to Thompson and Mrs. Thompson too on the way. Soon mother, son and lawyer were in a huddle by the bar.

It was seven months after the preliminary hearing, and there was a bargain to be made. The defender was convinced that a superior court jury would be too harsh on his client. He and the prosecutor had already met to exchange offers and counteroffers, and soon the judge would be in on it too. But, for then, it was between the defender and his client.

The defender spoke first, jerking his head up and down when he wanted to emphasize a point. "You can plead to a felony and get three years probation, no jail." (From my seat across the aisle I could make out the words.) "Or you can plead to a misdemeanor and get ninety days in jail, no probation." The defender was relaying the prosecutor's offer. The prosecutor himself was nowhere to be seen. He'd made an offer but he wasn't there to witness the dilemma it posed, for just as the defender was bound and determined to spare his client the hazards of probation, so the client was bound and determined to spare himself the agony of jail.

"No way!" Thompson tossed his head back in utter fury.

The defender waited before saying anything more. When he finally spoke, Thompson threw back his head again, and then the defender turned in desperation to Mrs. Thompson who took a long deep breath. "Son, I can't tell you what to plead. You've got to make that decision for yourself." Mrs. Thompson's deep voice was a wail filling the courtroom.

Before long court was in session. The prosecutor was present. Thompson was standing with his lawyer before the judge. Mrs. Thompson was three rows back in the spectators' section.

"I understand there's been an agreement between the district attorney and the defense lawyer," the judge said. "If the defendant enters a plea of guilty, the defendant won't go to prison. He will be referred to the probation officer."

"I want the record to reflect that another alternative was offered to Mr. Thompson," the defender said quietly, his head nodding almost imperceptibly as he looked squarely at the judge.

The judge peered over his glasses to return the stare. "The other alternative is that he could plead guilty to a misdemeanor and receive ninety days..."

Yes. The defender's nod was more pronounced.

"Which would end it for all time. It would be a misdemeanor for all time. He would go to jail and it would be over. Because if he is placed on probation now, if he doesn't go to jail and his probation is revoked later on, he could end up in the state penitentiary."

"I want the record to reflect that I have strongly recommended to Mr. Thompson that he plead guilty to the misdemeanor for ninety days, in terms of the entire impact on his record in the future," the defender said. He was nodding again, and the judge was nodding too.

The judge let his glasses dangle on a string around his neck. He bent forward across his desk. He rested his chin on his arms. He squinted and studied Mr. Thompson up and down.

Mr. Thompson shifted his weight from one foot to another while the prosecutor rested on his spine, rapping a pencil on the arm of his chair.

"If Mr. Thompson knows he is going to behave himself and stay out of trouble," the judge said, "he's passing up doing more time. But he has to realize what he's stepping into. He's stepping out where his conduct for the next three years is going to be such that if he violates the law, and it doesn't have to amount to a new felony. It could be such a thing, for example, as refusing to report to the probation officer. It could be for such a thing as failing to get permission to change his residence. It could be for such a thing as refusing to make an effort to get himself a job or to go to school. All of those things could be conditions of probation. And if he refused to do things to better himself, then he can be brought back in front of me, and if I think it proper, he will have his future education in a state prison for a while."

The judge's words flew out. Thompson gripped the edge of the table with his hands, and the muscles along his shoulders quivered like feathers.

"But the key to *his* jail is going to be in *his* hands," the judge went on, settling back in his chair.

"Certainly," the defender agreed.

"It all depends on how he wants to walk it. If he goes out, tries his best and stays out of trouble, fine. If, on the other hand, he conducts himself otherwise, then this thing is sitting there, and it can carry him to prison without him committing a penitentiary offense to get there. Do you understand, Mr. Thompson?"

Thompson's skin was silver with perspiration. He whispered

something to his lawyer. He and his lawyer sat down, leaving the judge's words hanging in air, tiny bits collecting into the shape of a large, quivering bird.

I'd read about the bird, a beautiful bird, a silver eagle. Balinese hunters had caught it. They'd shot a bullet into its eye. Priests had received the flawed animal. They'd taken it to a deserted spot and they'd sacrificed it to their gods, asking for an end to the world's disasters. (How the animal must have clawed and thrashed before his throat was cut!)

Calvin Thompson was a sacrifice. The policemen had caught him. They'd charged him with a crime. They'd delivered him to court where officials had received him, making ready for the sacrifice — Thompson in exchange for power. From a seat in the spectators' section, Mrs. Thompson looked on. Her expression said she'd expected everything that was happening, she'd been preparing for it from the day her son was born. From the day he'd taken his first steps, letting go of her hand, she'd known there were hunters in the darkness training their sights on her son.

"Mr. Thompson now feels, your honor, that he would rather plead to the misdemeanor and get the ninety days." The defender stood, and so did his client.

The judge transferred some papers from his desk to a manila folder, then slapped the folder shut.

"It's your time, mister," he told Thompson, "and the reason that I am taking the time with you is because I want you to understand and give you the opportunity to ask questions. Do you understand that you don't have to plead guilty to anything at this time because you have a right to a jury trial?"

"Yes," Thompson murmured.

"Do you understand you have a right to have the witnesses brought here in court?" the judge went on.

"Yes."

"And do you understand that you don't have to convict yourself out of your own mouth?"

"Yes."

"Now, has anybody threatened you in any fashion . . ."

Part III: The Altar

10

The People v. Marvin Washington

Marvin Washington was near the water fountain, surrounded by supporters. Reporters formed a group by the elevators, fifteen feet away. The hallway echoed with everyone's laughter.

A bailiff in a short sleeved shirt came out of one of the courtrooms and stood framed in the doorway. He was a big burly man with hairy arms, who wore a gun in a holster hanging from his belt. "Court is in session. Can we have a little quiet here, Mr. Washington," he called out, glowering.

PRELIMINARIES

In calendar court everyone was growing restless waiting for the judge to come out and assign the courtroom for Marvin Washington's trial.

The press had preempted the jury box. A matron had to ask a reporter to move so she and her two prisoners had somewhere to sit. Lawyers were jammed around the bailiff's desk. Indeed, the press seemed to have taken over the whole room. There were reporters to my left and to my right and behind me, and I recognized the man from Channel Five and the woman from Channel Seven way in the back of the room. Everyone was twisting and turning in their seats,

113

extending greetings, many hadn't seen each other since the last big trial.

Conversations were excited and hard to follow, although I didn't have to hear much to know the drift. Marvin Washington, who was back in Oakland after three years in exile, was going to stand trial on the charge of beating Henry Billings, the tailor. His trial was supposed to be like the second half of John Ramsey's trial, except that recently Billings had announced on TV that he was going to refuse to testify against Washington. He'd implied that it was Ramsey who had beaten him, and everyone was trying to guess how the prosecutor could possibly make a case without Billings for a witness, since Billings was the only prosecution witness who had seen the fight. There was a lot of talk about a recent magazine article claiming that Washington had bought Billings off, and reporters were discussing recent news stories quoting the prosecutor as saying that Billings had changed his story because he feared for his life. Behind me two black lawyers were saying the trial was another example of the harassment of Washington and the Commoners.

The prosecutor was the same one from John Ramsey's trial, the same one who over the years had tried a number of Commoners. He was leaning back in his chair at the lawyers' table, staring at the ceiling, smiling to himself, blowing smoke rings into the air. At one point he turned around to say hello to a pressman he knew. Then he stood up and paced back and forth. He tossed the bailiff an imaginary ball. He blew more smoke rings into the air.

Across the room lawyers poured out of the judge's office. The bailiff called court into session, and the judge entered and sat down at his desk. He read out Marvin Washington's name. Someone shouted that Washington was outside in the hallway. The judge read another name from his list.

An artist in shirt sleeves was in the jury box sketching the judge. In fact, there were three artists at their drawing pads. I recognized Washington's wife in the audience. Finally Washington himself came into the courtroom, his slender brown face set off by a wide halo of hair. He stopped at the back of the room to clasp the outstretched hand of an admirer, and then sat down beside his wife. A few minutes later the judge read his name again and told him to report to Courtroom J for trial.

The prosecutor lingered behind the railing, ringed by lawyers and reporters.

Washington left the courtroom flanked by comrades.

Reporters gathered in a circle in the hallway outside Courtroom J, passing time while the judge and the lawyers met in the judge's office, setting up ground rules for the trial. A black reporter, the only black reporter I'd seen till then, came out of the elevator.

"Well, Jim's here. We can start now." A reporter grinned at him.

"Hey, Bob. What've you been up to?" Jim joined the circle, slapping Bob's arm.

"Oh, I covered the Milligan trial last month."

"Oh? Which one was that?"

"The one with the little boy?"

Jim shook his head.

"The man and woman who killed the little boy?"

"Oh, yeah. Wow!"

"That's nothing," a reporter behind Jim chimed in. He had a Santa Claus beard, and his nose was buried in his moustache, so all you could see were his eyes. "The last case I covered, the woman was blind, and he raped her, and then he poked out her eye."

"They probably let him go, too," another male voice joined the chorus. "Like a few years ago this guy tied up this old woman in the kitchen, and then he popped her dog in the oven, and then he raped her. They let him go."

"This is the case of the people of the state of California versus Marvin Washington." The words rang out. A man in the second row slapped together the covers of the book he had been reading. A woman with fiery red hair and thick makeup choked back a laugh and blushed. Another woman started playing with her necklace, and her mouth twitched into a smile.

The judge dusted off his desk with the back of his hand. He settled into the black leather chair. "Our sole purpose today is to select a fair and impartial jury," he said, staring at the panelists in the jury box and in the audience. Under fluorescent lights his skin was silvery. His white hair shone.

The judge read off the charges against Washington. He read so slowly it sounded like more charges than there actually were: one charge of assault with a deadly weapon against Billings; two charges of illegally possessing a gun. The gun charges were being lodged, the judge explained, because Washington was an ex-felon, and ex-felons aren't allowed guns.

The judge explained that the jury would presume Washington was innocent until the prosecutor proved that he wasn't. He said it was the solemn duty, the sacred duty, of all jurors to follow the law as he explained it. Lacing his fingers together in front of his face, he let his voice trail off, and the courtroom filled with murmuring. Washington, in gray pants and a black velvet jacket, leaned forward to whisper something to one of his two lawyers.

"All right, now," the judge called out, and the courtroom was still. "If you've heard or read about this case before coming to this courtroom, raise your hand," he told the twelve women and men seated in the jury box.

All but four hands went up.

"Do any of you have an opinion in your mind as to whether Marvin Washington is guilty or innocent?" the judge asked the panelists.

Mr. Davis in seat number one raised his hand.

"Now, Mr. Davis, I don't want to know your opinion," the judge said, "but can you assure me you'll set it aside and listen to the evidence and make your verdict solely on the basis of the facts and the law?"

"Yes," Mr. Davis replied. The judge paused for a moment, and then Mr. Long in seat number four raised his hand and said he also had an opinion, but like Mr. Davis he was sure he could set it aside.

"All right. I'm going to permit the attorneys to question you." The judge nodded at the prosecutor who smiled and said he had no questions. He was sitting next to his black assistant, his arm draped over the back of his chair.

The defender got up and walked around the lawyers' table to face the jury. He was a tall, square man in his early sixties with thick white hair and bright blue eyes. Unsmiling, he stared at Mr. Davis.

"Mr. Davis, how long ago did you form your opinion?" the defender asked.

"When I read about it in the paper."

"Which paper?"

"The *Dispatch*."

In the spectators' section, the reporter from the *Star* poked the reporter from the *Dispatch* who was sitting beside him.

"Have you told anyone your opinion?" the defender asked.

"No," Mr. Davis replied.

"How would you vote right now?"

"I don't want to say."

"You can't ask that," said the judge.

"Yes, I can!" the defender wheeled around. "He's supposed to presume Mr. Washington is innocent!"

"All right," the judge murmured. He toyed with a sheet of paper on his desk. The *Star* reporter gaped at the judge, and one of the artists flipped over a page of his drawing pad and began furiously drawing the defender.

The defender turned and stared some more at Mr. Davis.

"I don't really have an opinion," Mr. Davis finally said.

"Does my client have a strike against him?" the defender asked.

"He's already answered," said the judge.

The defender stepped to his left so his back was to the judge.

"Mr. Davis," he said, "do you believe everything you read in the paper?"

"No, you can't ask that," the judge interrupted.

"Do you believe everything the state says?"

"Object," the prosecutor called out softly.

"Sustained," said the judge.

The defender heaved a great sigh and fastened his eyes on the man in seat number four. "Mr. Long?"

"If I voted right now, I'd vote guilty."

"But that would violate his honor's instructions that you're supposed to presume that Mr. Washington is innocent."

Mr. Long didn't reply.

"If you or your family were on trial, would you want someone like you on the jury?"

"Object."

"Sustained."

The defender abruptly turned and went to the judge's desk. Slowly the prosecutor got to his feet. The defender's associate was whispering something to Washington. Washington nodded, and the associate got up to join the lawyers. So did the prosecutor's assistant.

"I don't see why he's objecting so much," I could hear the man behind me whisper.

"Yeah," a woman replied. "I hope I don't get called. I'd like a short trial, just for the experience, don't you know, but this one's going to go on for months."

It seemed to me too that it was going to be a very long trial. The judge and the two principal lawyers were only displaying their colors. The main event was to come, although the excitement level already was higher than I'd ever experienced at any other trial.

To save two of his free challenges, the defender was trying to get the judge to excuse Mr. Davis and Mr. Long for legal cause, but he didn't seem to be having much success. After the men broke out of their huddle and the judge announced that he wasn't going to dismiss either man because both had promised to set aside their opinions, the defender took up his position in front of the jury box for one last question.

"Mr. Long, can you be fair?" the defender asked.

"No," Mr. Long answered.

The judge took off his glasses and peered at Mr. Long. "All right, if you can't be fair, you'll have to be excused." The judge rubbed his eyes, and he put on his glasses. "Now, does any other juror have in his mind, and of course when I say his mind I also mean her mind, that he couldn't be fair?" No hands went up. The judge continued his questioning. Jury selection lasted two and a half days. The prosecutor's questions went quickly enough — he asked a lot of panelists which newspapers they read, whether anyone was afraid of guns — but the defender's questions were long and tough. Where the prosecutor addressed the panel from behind the long table, his hands below his chin as if he were praying, the defender presented himself in full view, scowling, smiling, laughing, gesturing, talking in a folksy sort of twang. "Have you read any of Marvin Washington's essays? Have you heard about the Commoners' school? Do you have any quarrel with Marvin Washington having a bodyguard? Do you think people have a right to self-defense? If the evidence shows the bodyguard did it, will you hold Marvin responsible? Have you heard about the congressional committee investigating police infiltration into the Commoner Movement? Have you heard of a campaign on the part of law enforcement agencies to destroy Washington and the Commoners?"

Although the jury turned out to be predominantly white and suburban like the other juries I'd seen, the defender was able to use *voir dire* to raise issues, to build an image, to create a mood. Indeed, the prosecutor's frequent objections and the frequent conferences at the judge's desk made the defender's claims of a conspiracy against the Commoners seem all the more believable.

THE TRIAL

The trial of Marvin Washington was unlike any I'd ever seen. It wasn't only the sensationalism, having everything blown up bigger than life, although that certainly made a difference. It was that a story never really evolved. There never was an orderly unravelling, a beginning, middle, an end. Instead there were seemingly unrelated episodes, disjointed skirmishes, battles really, over the law.

Even the introduction was a battle. The prosecutor made his opening remarks to the jury, smiling boyishly. He told the jurors that Henry Billings was a distinguished sort of man. He told them how Billings met Washington and how he'd gone to Washington's apartment to fit Washington for clothes. He described how Billings called Washington baby, and how Washington got so mad he smashed Billings' head, and how Billings landed in the hospital with three fractures. He described Washington's apartment, and he showed the jury pictures the police took after the fight, colored photos of walls and carpets — great splotches of dried blood.

The defender made his opening presentation right after the prosecutor, not waiting until it was time for the defense as other defenders I'd seen had done. Perhaps he wanted the jurors to know right off that there was another side to the story. He told them the fight actually had been between Billings and Ramsey, and he probably wanted that alternative planted firmly in their minds. He said Billings was a surly sort of man who was cheating on his boss. He said he had arrived at Washington's apartment that Saturday morning three sheets to the wind, so drunk he'd hit Washington and come on to Washington's wife. He said John Ramsey had stepped in to protect Washington. He'd pistolwhipped Billings so hard Washington had had to pull him away. The defender said Ramsey was Washington's bodyguard. He said Ramsey was a frightening man, six feet eight inches tall, 350 pounds.

*　*　*

"This harassment has to stop!" The defender's associate burst into the courtroom. The morning recess was just over, and he was standing in the rear, shouting and waving his arms. "I was talking to one of the Commoners who's working on the defense, and an officer came up and said he wanted to talk to him, and he told me to go away. I told him I was his attorney, but the officer said he didn't care. Then he used his walkie-talkie to call headquarters and run a warrant check on him, right there in the hallway!"

The judge blanched as jurors and people in the audience turned their heads to stare. "Marvin's been stopped three times in the past five days by officers with drawn guns. This harassment has got to stop!" the associate said, coming down the aisle.

"There will be no harassment in this courtroom. I will look into this immediately," the judge murmured. Descending from his desk, he swept into his office, four lawyers at his heels.

The scuttlebutt was that Officer Arthur Como's testimony was going to be crucial to the prosecution, and the courtroom was jammed. The prosecution had already presented witnesses who had seen Ramsey bringing Billings home. But Como was the officer who had answered the apartment manager's call for help and was supposed to have been the first one to have talked to Billings about the fight. The word was that Billings had told him that Washington did it, and as Como was being sworn in the reporter from KXAF whispered to me that if Billings carried out his threat and refused to testify, Como's testimony would be all the prosecution had to tie Washington to the beating. He said because Como's accusation was secondhand (Billings told him Washington did it) it was "hearsay," and therefore might not be admissible in court. I could see one of the artists drawing the defender as he bent over the lawyers' table and conferred with his associate and Washington.

Officer Como wore his hair cut short. His black shoes were shined to a high gloss. He told the prosecutor he'd been in his police car cruising in downtown Oakland the day Henry Billings was beaten. He said he'd responded to an ambulance request call from the manager of Billings' apartment house at about three forty or three forty-five. "Someone met me outside the apartment and took me inside the garage," he said. "I walked into the garage where I observed an individual lying on the floor right next to the elevator."

"What, if anything, unusual did you notice about this individual?" the prosecutor asked.

"I noticed that he was bleeding from the head. His clothes had a considerable amount of blood on them," Como responded.

"Did he appear to be in pain?"

"Yes. He was groaning. He was partially on the floor, sort of propped up against the wall."

"And did you ask him anything?"

"Yes. As nearly as I can recall, I said, 'Who did this?' or 'What happened to you?' "

"Now, yes or no, did he respond to that inquiry?" the prosecutor asked slowly.

Everyone — the clerk and the bailiff and the jurors and the reporters around me — everyone was staring in suspense at Como who answered yes.

"What did he tell you?" the prosecutor asked.

"Object! Hearsay!" The defender sprang to his feet, and the judge said mechanically, "All right, then. We'll take this up out of the presence of the jury." He told the jury not to speculate about what would be said in its absence and nodded at the bailiff who jumped up to open the side door so the jurors could leave.

"The judge's already made up his mind. It's clear," the man next to me with the handlebar moustache said as he nudged my arm with his elbow. "All of this now is just for the record." He was a lawyer from San Diego. I'd heard him tell the bailiff when he'd commandeered a press seat. "It was the testimony about the blood. You'll see," he told me.

"How's the judge going to rule?" I asked, even though I was sure I knew the answer.

"Oh, for the prosecution. This ruling is going to be crucial."

"Isn't Como's testimony hearsay?"

"It falls under an exception to the hearsay rule," he replied, waving me still.

"Now, Officer Como, do you know at what time Billings was assaulted?" It was the defender speaking. He was tense and his voice was strained.

"No, it's an estimate on my part," the officer replied.

"What specifically was your inquiry? Was it, 'Who did it?' or was it, 'What happened?' " the defender asked. The jury box was empty, so his questions were for the judge's benefit. They were part of his legal argument which he was getting into the record in case he needed it later for an appeal.

Officer Como replied that he couldn't remember precisely what he'd asked or verbatim what Billings had responded. He said he'd never written that down in his report.

"Did you take notes when Mr. Billings spoke to you?"

"Yes."

"Where are they?"

"I destroyed them after I wrote the report."

"Did you talk to anyone else before you wrote the report?"

"Yes, I believe I did. I talked to some of the other officers."

"So what you learned from Henry Billings and what you learned from the other officers is all kind of muddled now?"

"Objection."

"Sustained."

"You've already made up your mind! Why bother to continue?" the defender yelled at the judge.

"No, Mr. Defender, the court has *not* made up its mind. . . . I'll overrule the objection." The judge sounded angry and confused. A woman from the defender's office told me before the trial that the defender and the judge had known each other for a long time. I thought the defender was taking advantage of his personal knowledge of the judge.

When the defender finished questioning Como, the prosecutor presented his legal argument. He said since Billings was still bleeding and obviously still in pain when he talked to Officer Como, what he said was spontaneous.

"That's it!" the lawyer beside me whispered into my ear. "The whole issue is whether it was a spontaneous statement. That's the exception to the hearsay rule! If it's spontaneous, it's admissible. If Billings spoke in the heat of passion, right after he was beaten, then there wasn't time for him to make up a lie."

I scratched my forehead and started writing down what the lawyer had just said, and he peered over my shoulder, stopping me once to correct a mistake. Meanwhile the prosecutor was citing legal cases that he said supported his argument.

"Your honor, this is the most crucial point in the case! This may be the only direct evidence implicating Mr. Washington if Mr. Billings takes the Fifth!" the defender was shouting. "You can't find the statement was spontaneous because the prosecutor hasn't shown how much time elapsed between the assault and when Billings made the accusation!"

"Oh, yes I can!" cried the judge. "The blood was still wet."

"That's a smart judge. He's thinking," the lawyer beside me whispered.

"If the blood was wet it was spontaneous?"

"Yes. That shows how little time elapsed. It shows Billings spoke in the heat of passion."

"You're not serious? If the blood was wet, the statement is admissible? If the blood was dry, it isn't?"

"Why not?" the lawyer answered. "If the blood was wet, not much time had elapsed. Billings was still stunned by the beating Washington gave him. He wasn't likely to lie."

"But there was time to take him home, to call the police . . ."

The lawyer shrugged.

The hearsay rule, I'd been told, was supposed to protect defendants' constitutional right to confront their accusers, although the courts made exceptions when they thought the likelihood of the absent victim's testimony being false was exceedingly slim, when a dying man named his assailant, for instance. It was certainly possible that Billings had been so traumatized by his beating he hadn't had the capacity to lie, although I wasn't completely satisfied with his account of what had happened. If his coming on to Mrs. Washington *had* had something to do with the fight, as Washington claimed, I thought Billings would have found a way to lie. After all, when he talked to Officer Como he was on his way home to his wife. I didn't see how anyone could be as certain about Billings' state of mind as the lawyer seemed to be. Wet blood. Dry blood. In making up that rule, some judge must have been trying to be terribly scientific, but it sounded like witchcraft to me.

I wondered if the prosecutor was convinced of the logic of his own argument. I was sure that if it had suited his case, he would have argued the other side. I didn't think logic had much to do with what was happening. The prosecutor wanted Billings' statement before the jury, and he'd thrown out a rule to get it there. He'd thrown out a hoop for the defender to jump through, a dragon for the defender to slay.

The jurors came back into the courtroom, talking and smiling among themselves the way people do when they begin to get to know each other. The prosecutor asked Officer Como what Billings had told him, and Officer Como replied that Billings had said he went to Marvin Washington's apartment to fit him for clothes. "In the course of conversation Billings said he referred to Washington as baby, and Washington beat him on the head with a pistol, and he kicked him."

That was the officer's testimony. The defender cross examined briefly. Then the officer got up and left, smiling at the prosecutor on his way out. The judge excused the jury, and as one of the black jurors passed in front of Washington, she turned her head and looked the other way.

In the hallway, a young reporter eagerly told his senior colleagues, "I saw Washington at a jazz concert last week. He got up and made a speech."

"I don't know about you, but I'm not intelligent enough to understand his philosophy," a senior reporter said, chuckling. "It's like the theory of relativity."

"Yeah. It's not the train that's moving to the station, it's the station that's moving to the train," said another. Peals of laughter echoed in the hallway.

It was standing room only again in the courtroom the following afternoon. Near the doorway I recognized several men from the DA's office. The bailiff went up and down the aisle, making sure no one was blocking the way. Inside the bar sat the jurors and judge and lawyers and Washington. A man with red hair—I was sure he was Billings' lawyer—was in a chair near the side door. All at once, as though a signal had sounded, everyone stopped talking and heads turned to watch Henry Billings coming in through the courtroom door. Billings looked tired as he came down the aisle in a smart brown suit which set off his silver gray hair. He sounded tired when the clerk swore him in.

"Mr. Billings, how old are you?" the prosecutor began direct examination, making it sound as though he were asking an important question.

Billings glanced at his lawyer and then replied, "I'm fifty-six years old, sir."

"Are you married?" the prosecutor asked.

"Yes, about twenty-nine years, sir."

"Mr. Billings, above your right eyebrow I see what appears to be a scar. When did you receive the injury?"

Again Billings glanced at his lawyer. "Four years ago, sir," he said.

"On what date?"

Billings looked at his lawyer, and then he held up a scrap of paper from which he read, "I respectfully decline to answer on the grounds to do so might tend to incriminate me in violation of the Fifth Amendment."

There it was. Billings was refusing to testify. The *Dispatch* reporter got up and hurried out of the courtroom, and a lawyer from the DA's office who'd been watching from the back of the room left too, and a lot of people in the audience started whispering. Billings seemed lost in another world. If he did testify, and if he said it was Ramsey who attacked him, not Washington as he'd previously testified, then he'd be as much as admitting he lied under oath. The Fifth Amendment of the Constitution was supposed to protect him from such self-incrimination, although he certainly didn't *look* as though he felt protected. He looked as though he wished there was a world with no courtrooms or judges or DA's — or people named Marvin Washington.

"Mr. Billings, do you have a lawyer?" the judge asked quietly.

"I have a lawyer, sir." Billings motioned toward the man with red hair.

"So you've been advised to say what you're saying?"

"Yes, sir."

The judge looked down at the prosecutor who was standing just a few feet away from Billings. The prosecutor continued with his questions.

"Mr. Billings, four years ago did you testify in a preliminary hearing in a criminal case against a man named John Ramsey?"

Billings didn't respond.

"You can answer that. It's not incriminating," the judge told him gently.

"Yes, sir," Billings replied.

"Did you testify at the trial of John Ramsey?" the prosecutor asked.

"Yes, sir."

"And last spring at Marvin Washington's preliminary hearing?"

"Yes, sir."

The prosecutor moved around the lawyers' table to stand behind Marvin Washington. "Do you know this man?"

"I respectfully decline to answer on the grounds to do so might tend to incriminate me."

The prosecutor looked at the judge, and the judge motioned for the lawyers to follow him into his office.

"He's got everything he needs now," the lawyer from San Diego whispered as he peered over my arm to see what I was writing.

"Who has?" I asked, clicking back the point of my pen.

"The prosecutor. He's got Como's testimony and Billings' behavior right now. That's all the jury needs. It's clear Washington is intimidating him, the way he testified all those times before and now suddenly he's scared."

"Maybe the jury will think it's because Billings isn't very reliable." I reminded the lawyer that the first day of the trial the neurosurgeon had testified that Billings was so drunk when he arrived at the hospital he was on the verge of the DT's.

"No. It's clear Billings is taking orders from the defender."

I had to agree that that was precisely what everyone might think. I found it hard to imagine myself that something hadn't transpired between Billings and Washington. "What do you think the defender wants Billings to do?" I asked.

"To keep quiet," the lawyer answered. "If Billings gets up there and says Ramsey did it, the prosecutor can use all of his previous testimony to impeach him. That's the problem. It'd do more harm for Billings to get up there and say Washington's innocent because then the jury would hear about all the times he said Washington was guilty." He was resting on his spine and his hands were on his stomach. "It's like a war, you know. You have to measure each step you take because what may be to your advantage here and now may get you killed further down the line."

"You mean if Billings doesn't testify, there's no way the prosecutor can let the jury know about the previous testimony?"

"Well, not exactly," the lawyer winked. "Let's say it would complicate things."

"But it wouldn't make it impossible?"

"Not impossible."

It was Friday afternoon, the fourth day of the trial, three days after the prosecutor had begun presenting the material evidence. He'd shown the jury the pictures the police took in Washington's apartment after the fight, and he'd fished into I don't know how many paper bags for bloody guns and bloody towels and bloody clothing. He'd even unrolled a huge piece of bloody carpet from Washington's apartment for the jury to see. By the time he got around to Washington's bloody jeans, I was yawning, and juror number four was reaching into her blouse to adjust her bra strap, and juror number ten was swiveling around in his chair. The defender's associate stood to say he hoped the prosecutor wasn't planning to bring in the blood stained toilet too, and juror number three laughed, but the rest of the jurors didn't. They just looked bored.

The reporter from KXAF and I rehashed the testimony during intermissions, and we agreed that the prosecutor had proved that someone pistolwhipped Billings in Washington's apartment, but he hadn't proved who. The reporter said he was disturbed by the way the trial was going. He said he thought the prosecutor was taking so much time presenting the material evidence because he wanted Billings' appearance to fall on Friday afternoon when the judge could threaten to put him in jail over the long Labor Day weekend if he refused to testify. He said he'd always thought trials were supposed to be rational procedures and he was bothered by the strong-arm tactics on both sides.

I recalled his theory just then because, as we were waiting for the judge and lawyers, two extra bailiffs came down the aisle and took up posts at the side door.

After the judge and lawyers came back to the courtroom, the prosecutor presented the judge with a written request for immunity for Billings. The judge read it aloud. Then he announced that Billings was no longer in danger of self incrimination and could be legally held in contempt of court and put in jail if he refused to testify. This was what everyone had expected. I was sure Billings' lawyer had told him to expect it too.

"But I don't think that's full immunity!" the reporter from KXAF whispered. "He just said he wouldn't prosecute Billings for his *past* lies."

"His past lies?" I asked.

"Yeah," the lawyer from San Diego broke in. "Billings can be held to answer for any lies he tells after he's granted immunity."

"Then if Billings says Ramsey beat him, the prosecutor can say he's lying and prosecute him for that?" I asked.

The lawyer grinned.

"Billings is supposed to be the victim, but I don't think anyone up there cares what happens to him. They're having too much fun," the reporter from KXAF said.

I told him I agreed. Billings was being used. Both sides were batting him about like a shuttlecock. If the prosecutor needed a distinguished gentleman, that's what Billings was. If he needed a criminal who was obstructing justice, Billings was that, or the surly individual the defender portrayed, or the victim. I agreed, no one cared about Billings, although I didn't think anyone was having fun. Too much was at stake.

The reporter nodded. He said Washington was convinced the police were out to get him, and he was fighting for his life.

I said it seemed to me that the prosecutor was fighting for his life too, and the moment I said it I realized that this trial was the first real contest I'd seen since I'd begun covering the courthouse. Other defendants had been so passive. But Washington, flanked by two lawyers, exuded power. He was giving the prosecutor a run for his money.

The judge handed the prosecutor's request for immunity to the clerk who picked up a rubber stamp from a corner of her desk, then slammed it down.

"All right, now, the prosecutor will proceed," the judge said.

Once again the prosecutor moved directly behind Marvin Washington: "Do you know this man?"

Once again Billings refused to answer, explaining that he didn't think he was really immune from prosecution.

"All right, the jury will be excused," the judge said, and he hurried off to his office.

"One of the lawyers told me he keeps running to his office to watch the ball game." The reporter from KXAF grinned.

A few minutes later the judge was back at his desk asking Billings if he'd changed his mind. No, Billings replied, he didn't mean to be disrespectful, but he didn't believe he was really immune.

"No district attorney can grant you immunity for anything you might say in the future which might be perjurious."

Billings stared dumbly at the judge.

"I will detain him until he does testify," the judge was speaking to Billings' lawyer.

"Yes, he's asking for a license to commit perjury," the prosecutor concurred. "The courts have continually said that the oath is sacred. We don't give a license for perjury."

"But even if what he testifies to is true, if the prosecutor believes he committed perjury, he can charge him," Billings' lawyer said.

"It's not my function to advise you about that," the judge said, and he stood up. "I'll put this case over and let you think about it, and I'll put your client in custody."

"Isn't there some way the court could resolve this?" the defender broke in.

The judge squinted at him through the top part of his glasses. He sat back down.

"Isn't there some way that the prosecutor can be prevented from using Mr. Billings' old lies against him in a perjury proceeding?" the defender suggested. What he was really requesting was a promise not to prosecute Billings at all. He was asking the judge to rule that the prosecutor couldn't use any of Billings' prior testimony against him, which would mean there wouldn't be any way to prove that the second version of his story was a lie.

The prosecutor gazed up at the ceiling. "I could research that to see if I can do it legally and ethically," he said. Grinning at the judge, he added, "I would like in my heart of hearts to have the benefit of Mr. Billings' testimony."

"So would I, your honor," the defender declared.

"Well, if there *is* perjury, you can't *not* prosecute, but he will only be prosecuted if there *is* perjury," said the judge. "Ours is a government of laws. At any rate I'm not going to let him loose today. I'm going to put him in custody. I'm glad both attorneys want him to testify."

"Your honor!" the defender and Billings' lawyer were crying out at once.

"I object to your putting him in jail over a long weekend when it's not decided!" yelled the defender.

"Why shouldn't he go into custody when he flouts the order of this court?" Now it was the judge who was angry.

"Because he's been sick!" Mrs. Billings called out from the audience and the judge started. Mrs. Billings was in the press row, several seats to my left, over by the wall. I'd noticed her earlier, with her graying hair, but I hadn't realized who she was.

"This is coercion, plain and simple!" Billings' lawyer cried out.

"If I'm in error, the appellate courts are open. Take it to them." The judge glared at Billings' lawyer.

"I'm appealing to your fairness, your honor. The DA hasn't had time to consider this," Billings' lawyer replied softly.

"Mr. Billings is disobeying the lawful order of this court. The judge has no other way to make him testify!" The prosecutor sounded angrier than I'd ever heard him sound.

"We don't want the court to punish him when it may do no good," the defender said.

"Ours is a government of laws, and we can't have lawful orders disobeyed!" the judge cried. He called the jury back into the courtroom to listen to the prosecutor ask Billings the same questions again, and when Billings refused to answer, the judge sent the jury home and Billings upstairs to jail. As the bailiff was closing the side door, the prosecutor stood up and he shook his assistant's hand. Then he stepped over to a senior member of the DA's staff who was sitting on the sidelines and patted him on the back. The defender and his associate were still at the lawyers' table, their heads together. In the audience, Mrs. Billings cried.

"You don't think the defender has changed his mind, do you? You don't think he really wants Billings to testify?" I asked the lawyer beside me.

"Nah. He's just playing games, sounding fair for the record."

"That's what I think too."

"The question now is whether the prosecutor will call his bluff."

"Would you?"

"Probably." He grinned.

"You said you do defense work in San Diego?"

"Yes," the lawyer replied.

"You seem to understand the prosecution strategy well too."

"Oh, I used to be in the DA's office in San Diego. I've done both," he told me. Then, seeing the look of amusement on my face, he shrugged. "You play to win, you know. You can do that from either side."

*   *   *

"Would you bring Mr. Billings in, please," the judge called out. It was Tuesday morning. The bailiff left by the side door and went up the narrow stairway, leaving the door open while the spectators quieted down. There were a few isolated coughs, and from far off in the stairwell you could hear the faint echo of voices and the sound of footsteps coming closer. Billings came out looking less well groomed than he had on Friday. He was straightening his jacket, pulling down the cuffs of his shirt, fixing his collar.

"It's okay with me," the prosecutor began. "I'll promise not to use any of his prior statements against him in any proceeding."

"That in effect would mean he couldn't be charged with perjury," said the judge.

"The practical effect would be to make it impossible to prosecute him for perjury," the prosecutor agreed. The prosecutor cited the McGee case, or the Medina case—there was so much excited whispering in the audience I was having trouble hearing—which he said outlawed putting undue pressure on someone to testify.

"And now what happens to Marvin Washington's rights if you give Billings a license to lie?" It was the defender.

"Wasn't it the defender who suggested not using Billings' prior statements against him?" I asked the reporter from KXAF who was sitting next to me again.

"That's what I thought," he replied.

"Mr. Defender, do you want this witness to testify?" the judge asked angrily.

"Of course I do, but not with a license to lie, knowing full well that if he does tell the truth he won't be prosecuted."

"It was the defender's suggestion that we look into this compromise. This is exactly what he suggested on Friday!" the prosecutor cried.

"I said on Friday I wanted Billings to tell the truth!"

"Are you afraid now that the man will change his story again and say what he said at the other trials?" The judge was grinning.

"If the man is given a license to lie, you're depriving Mr. Washington of his rights. This is not a laughing matter."

"What I want is a promise my client won't be prosecuted," Billings' lawyer chimed in.

"How could he possibly be prosecuted?" the judge asked.

"I want to talk to my client," Billings' lawyer said.

"All right, I'll recess until tomorrow so you can talk to him."

"There's no need for a recess!" the defender yelled. "Do it now! You're using your power illegally to stall, and you're intimidating Billings. You're denying my client a fair and speedy trial. You should ask Billings if there's any chance he'll testify. See if there's any point to keeping him in jail."

"I'll put it over a few days, and we can have a hearing."

"I can tell you right now my client won't testify." It was Billings' lawyer.

"How do you know that?" the judge asked.

"He told me just now while you and the defender were arguing."

"He won't testify even if the prosecutor won't use the prior statements against him?"

"No."

"You want to give him a license to lie!"

"Oh, Mr. Defender, how clever you are," murmured the judge.

The argument continued that way for quite a while. I felt like I was watching a tennis match where players were furiously leaping from one side of the net to the other, playing both sides:

"I can't give him a license to lie!" The prosecutor slams the ball with a powerful forehand.

"It's not a license to lie." The defender returns the shot.

Both men hurdle the net. Then, from their new sides: "It's perfectly legal and ethical after all." (The prosecutor)

"No, no it isn't. You're giving him a license to lie!" (The defender)

The sound is squeaky: biddy biddy bee, biddy biddy bee, and movements are disjointed, a fast motion film.

"You're playing games with my client!" Billings' lawyer called out to the judge. "He wouldn't even be here if it weren't Marvin Washington on trial. All the time across the land witnesses are backing down or changing their stories and DA's dismiss the cases. You're punishing Billings because the defendant has a high profile."

"That's not true, sir. This trial isn't any different from any other trial," the judge replied, and he adjourned until the next day, sending a message upstairs with the bailiff for the jury to go home.

By then the jury had been out of the courtroom more than it had been in.

The judge asked Billings himself whether or not he would testify. No, Billings replied, not under any circumstances. People had been hassling him about this case for years, he said, and he wanted it over and done with.

The judge ordered Billings jailed for the duration of the trial, saying, "Justice demands it. The lawful orders of this court must be obeyed. That's the whole basis of due process."

I underlined that statement after I wrote it down.

Following Billings' incarceration there came a great legal debate that lasted a full day. The question was whether any of Billings' prior statements were admissible evidence now that it was clear he wasn't going to testify. The jury spent the whole time upstairs, and the spectators' section, which was pretty full at first, rapidly emptied out. Only a few reporters stayed. Even Washington was out of the courtroom most of the time.

As I understood it, the judge was going to allow the prosecutor to read to the jury Billings' testimony from Washington's preliminary hearing because Washington himself had been there, and he'd had the chance to cross examine his accuser, a right guaranteed him by the Constitution. The trouble was, though, that Billings hadn't said very much. He'd answered questions like, yes, he'd once had waffles and bacon when lunching with the prosecutor. But with one exception he'd answered the questions about what had happened in Washington's apartment by saying, "I don't remember."

The exception was that Billings had said he was hit from behind, so he never saw his assailant. Since that contradicted what he supposedly told Officer Como and since it favored the defense, the prosecutor argued that the jury had to hear all of Billings' testimony from John Ramsey's trial in order to weigh these two contradictory statements. The defender argued that that would be unconstitutional because Washington hadn't been at the trial to challenge any of Billings' accusations. The prosecutor countered that it didn't matter since the testimony wouldn't be offered for whether it was true or not but solely to discredit Billings' subsequent statements.

All of this the lawyer beside me patiently explained, and all of this I wrote down, only to have to read and reread it again because I kept losing the logic. One minute I would think I understood, but then like a dream it would slip out of my head. It seemed terribly odd to me that the prosecutor would introduce evidence favorable to the defense and then argue that he should be allowed to use otherwise inadmissible evidence to impeach the statement he himself introduced. Apparently the defender agreed with me. He said the prosecutor was setting up his own straw man, then beating it half to death.

He was red faced and terribly angry, and there was a lot of shouting and yelling back and forth between him and the judge who was reddening too, and even the prosecutor lost his temper. The judge adjourned early, saying he wanted time to consider the lawyers' arguments. This was new legal ground, he said.

When the judge announced that he was going to let the prosecutor read all of Billings' prior testimony to the jury, the defender slumped in his chair and stared out the window. The defender's associate whispered something to Washington, but Washington didn't respond. He seemed to wilt too.

The jury came down from the jury room, and the prosecutor introduced an investigator from his office who he said would take the stand to read Billings' part, to sort of break up the testimony and make it more understandable. The investigator was an older black man, like Billings.

"I want to object to the reading of this testimony. Its sole purpose is to prejudice this jury against my client." The defender said for the benefit of the jury.

The prosecutor picked up a transcript and opened it up and began reading what he'd asked at Washington's preliminary hearing: "Did we have lunch together?" He sounded wooden reading his own words.

"Yes, I had waffles and bacon," the investigator replied with expression, talking right into the mike, holding his copy of the transcript out in front of him and slightly to the side, like an actor reading a script.

"Did you go to Marvin Washington's apartment in August four years ago?"

"Yes."

"And did Marvin Washington pistolwhip you?"

"They hit me from the rear. I never seen the party that struck me."

"Didn't you say at John Ramsey's trial, 'Marvin Washington was mad at me for calling him baby?' "

"I don't remember."

"Didn't you say at John Ramsey's trial, 'Marvin Washington hit me over the head with a pistol?' "

"I don't remember."

"Didn't you say at John Ramsey's trial, 'He hit me so hard it broke my partial?' "

"I don't remember."

I realized that during Washington's preliminary hearing the prosecutor had been doing just what he was doing now: reading into the record Billings' previous testimony. I was listening to a transcript within a transcript, to a play within a play.

"Didn't you say at John Ramsey's trial, 'I was bleeding so badly I couldn't see?' " the prosecutor read.

"I don't remember," the investigator read back.

The judge intervened to remind the jury that since Billings hadn't answered most of the prosecutor's questions, except to say I don't remember, the testimony had no probative value. It wasn't being offered for whether it was true but only to discredit Billings' one substantive statement, that he never saw who hit him. I wrote all that down in my notebook again, and then I wrote: How can the jury use Billings' statements to discredit the claim that he never saw his assailant, unless they decide that the statements were true?

The reading continued on through the afternoon and into the next day when the prosecutor and his investigator, joined by the prosecutor's black assistant taking the part of Ramsey's black lawyer, did the transcripts from Ramsey's preliminary hearing, and then from Ramsey's trial. It meant that everyone heard the same lines two times again. As the men read on, the few reporters still in the courtroom whispered among themselves, the lone remaining artist sketched the investigator in his checkered jacket and red tie (an outfit Billings never would have worn), the court reporter tapped away on her little machine, unreeling yards and yards of paper tape, and a man sitting behind me yawned out loud.

At 11:03 ("I went to Washington's apartment... I called him baby...") juror number twelve, an older woman in a powder blue pantsuit, popped a lifesaver into her mouth, and juror number six, a younger man with a short natural, twiddled his thumbs. At 11:06 ("He whacked me and kicked me in the stomach...") juror number nine reached under his jacket to scratch his shoulder, and juror number three tilted her chair back against the wall and gazed at the ceiling. At 11:32 ("Blood was everywhere... I was bleeding like a pig... I think he went through my skull...") juror number three closed her eyes. So did the bailiff.

After lunch I sat near the aisle—there was no trouble finding a seat—and watched the prosecutor place a tape recorder on the witness chair. I guessed he was preparing to play the same tape he'd played at Ramsey's trial, the one of Billings moaning and gasping at the hospital, telling the police about the beating. The judge came out of his office. No sooner had he sat down than the defender's associate stood and started objecting.

The defender's associate was about twenty-five years younger than the defender, about the same age as the prosecutor. He was short and stocky and wore a moustache, and he told the judge that the tape would be the only thing in this trial with Billings' voice, which made it especially prejudicial.

"Well, I understood you were going to offer Billings' TV interview," the judge murmured, looking at the prosecutor who was placing a copy of the transcript of the tape on each juror's chair.

"There's no tape of the interview," the associate replied.

"Well, Billings is in custody upstairs. You can call him down. Whether or not he will testify for Mr. Washington, I don't know."

"You know as well as I do that the man isn't available!" Now the defender was up, and the associate was sitting. "This tape is blatantly prejudicial!"

"I know your technique, Mr. Defender," the judge mumbled. "Use words like blatant and outrageous over and again so people will believe it." Then, to the bailiff, "Call the jury."

The jurors came down and took their places while the defender and judge argued on. Then the defender sat down, and his associate stood up to argue some more, and it went on that way for some time, the defender and his associate taking turns, the defender yelling and getting all red, his associate talking more calmly, sort of a Mutt-and-Jeff routine.

"You're trying to convince this jury that the judge doesn't know what the law is," the judge cried. He looked down at his hands. Then he said softly, "Members of the jury, please disregard this colloquy. I know you're going to decide this case on the basis of the evidence." Again the judge explained that the tape wasn't being offered for the truth of what Billings had said but only to discredit his claim that he hadn't seen who hit him. "Does the jury understand what I said?" the judge asked.

Everyone in the jury box nodded yes.

Looking fresh and unruffled in a gray plaid suit, the prosecutor stood by the witness chair and, when it was absolutely still, he pushed a button, filling the courtroom with gasps and sighs: "I called him baby... kicked me in the face... blood in my eyes... No, I wasn't drunk...." Everyone was looking at the witness stand where the tape recorder was testifying.

The most unexpected event in the whole trial was also the briefest. The prosecution rested, the judge called for a recess, and after lunch the courtroom was jammed, standing room only. Everyone was waiting to see Washington begin the defense. If a hot dog vendor had come down the aisle, it wouldn't have surprised me.

The jury filed in. The defender rose. The courtroom was still. "The defense rests," the defender said and sat back down.

"They're not going to put up a defense?" the reporter from KXAF whispered hoarsely. Everyone else in the audience was whispering too, and so were the prosecutor and his assistant.

"I guess not," I replied.

"Will the jury please retire to the jury room," the judge called out. "Will counsel please come into my chambers." The judge's voice was shaking.

"Did you expect it?" the reporter asked me.

"No," I told him. I really hadn't, although when the trial began I'd wondered why the defender had made his opening presentation right after the prosecutor's. I realized he must have planned all along to forego the defense, and he'd gotten Washington's version of the fight before the jury while he could.

"Oh, they're making a terrible mistake," the reporter said. He sounded upset. "There won't be anything to counter all that testimony."

"Well, Washington isn't always so cool when he's talking in public. Maybe they were afraid to put him on the stand," I suggested, thinking of how disastrous it had been for Ramsey to testify.

The reporter shook his head. I wasn't convinced by my argument either. I decided I'd have to think about it later on. Right then there was too much of a commotion.

In the lobby, TV reporters circled around Washington, thrusting microphones attached to long black cords in front of his face. Cameramen positioned themselves around the reporters and aimed their cameras at Washington who buttoned his beige jacket and said he

thought this trial was just one more example of the power of the state
being lodged against him.

"Why didn't you put up a defense?" a reporter called out.

"The state's case is so flimsy we wouldn't grace it with a defense,"
Washington replied. His speech was clipped. He sounded nervous. I
realized it was the first time I'd heard him talk since the trial began.

Just then the judge passed by on his way down the hall with a
colleague. Turning to glare at Washington, he muttered, "Big
wheel."

THE VERDICT

After the lawyers made their closing arguments and the judge explained the law, the jurors retired to the jury room upstairs where
they deliberated from Monday through Friday before reaching a
verdict. They met from nine to five with time out for lunch. The rest
of the time they spent sequestered in a hotel.

Around the courtroom everyone played a waiting game. There
were a few reporters and artists, and there were defense lawyers and
defense staff (Washington was staying in a nearby apartment) and
the bailiff and the clerk, and a couple of Commoners and curious
onlookers. The phone kept ringing, and the clerk kept answering,
"Department J ... no, not yet."

It was a time to get to know one another. The bailiff told the
defender's associate about his kids, the clerk told a lawyer where she
had gone to college, reporters and artists took time together over
lunch, and much to everyone's delight artists drew pictures of people
in the courtroom. The judge, who spent the time sequestered in his
office, called in one of the artists each day to see his pictures. People
were reading—the sports section was especially popular—and
doing crossword puzzles and playing games. The reporter from
KXAF and I and two lawyers kept a word game going for half a day.

Everyone was taking bets on when the jury would have a verdict— toward the beginning of the week you had to guess the day,
later on, the hour—and of course we were all guessing which jurors
would vote which way. At first we were all sure the jury would
convict, but then some of us decided it was likely to hang. The
hanging theory seemed like the best bet by Wednesday when the
jury announced it had reached verdicts on the two gun charges, but

it was split ten to two on the assault. Over defense objections the judge had the jury go back upstairs to deliberate some more.

Although the jury wasn't allowed to say which way the votes had gone, everyone, except for a student I'd talked to, was sure it was for conviction. The student said that if he were a juror he'd be furious at the way the lawyers had played games with him, especially the prosecutor — trying to make him think he could listen to Billings' previous testimony four times through without considering whether or not it was true. He said he'd be so furious he'd vote to acquit. I told him I thought he had a point, but he was forgetting that he was dealing with a white suburban jury.

There was guessing about who the two holdouts on the jury were, but it was hard to carry that very far because the jurors had been in the jury room for most of the trial, and no one had much of a sense of knowing them. The college professor, juror number six, seemed to me to have been very attentive to the prosecutor, and the student, juror number eleven, had seemed to want it all over and done with so she could get back to school, and the warehouseman had worn a determined made-up-his-mind look through most of the trial. I guessed those three would be on the side to convict. The black man and woman were the ones everyone was saying would do the hanging, but the woman had made such a point of looking away every time she passed by Washington, I wasn't at all sure about her. So what the jury would end up doing was a mystery which people wondered about as they whiled away the time with games.

We all knew Friday was going to be the day. Late in the morning the courtroom came alive. People began dropping in: Commoners, lawyers, the prosecutor too, from his office upstairs. Everyone wanted to know what was going on.

In the afternoon Washington arrived. He walked down the aisle, he danced really, taking short steps, abruptly bending over to greet a follower, laughing, an uneven nervous laugh, shaking someone's hand. He hugged a woman on the defender's staff; he cracked a joke; he talked to the defender who was waiting in the jury box. The defender asked him if he wanted to go to the bar across the street for a drink. Washington said yes.

There was no doubt it was the day. Everyone agreed the judge wouldn't sequester the jury over the weekend, especially after the

defender had made such an issue of the sequestering altogether. It
had been the defender's associate, actually, who'd protested, charging the judge and prosecutor with creating an atmosphere of fear,
making the jury feel it needed protection, the sequestering coming
so soon after the prosecutor announced in his closing argument that
he thought Billings had refused to testify because he feared for his
life.

As I watched Washington going back up the aisle, stopping again
to talk with friends, I realized how taut his body was. I'd overheard
the defender telling an assistant earlier that he'd warned Washington
to expect a conviction. So I knew Washington was prepared to lose,
but it wasn't until I saw his lips quivering as though he were in pain,
that I realized he was nervous. The image flashed through my mind
again of the great silver bird, its feathers rippling, priests carrying it
off to slit its throat. It was an incredible association.

Washington and the defender left the courtroom, the defender's
hand on Washington's shoulder. More people came in — more artists
and reporters. The first row was full and the bailiff blocked off a
second row of seats for the press. Washington's family and supporters were in the audience. There were a lot of lawyers too. Soon many
were standing in the back of the room. Everyone was talking and
their voices echoed, making the courtroom seem larger. The prosecutor came in, followed by a senior member of the DA's staff who
took a seat inside the bar, a seat previously reserved for a lawyers'
assistant, now reserved for a dignitary. I stared at the two men
talking and joking. I heard their laughter over the din. What a
spectacle this was! I might have been at the Roman Colosseum.

I recalled the prosecutor telling the jury at John Ramsey's trial
that Marvin Washington was a mean and vicious man. His voice had
trembled and his eyes had narrowed as though he were convinced
that half the evil in the world was contained in Washington's slender
body. I suddenly realized that it wasn't Washington who was on
trial. It was a man turned into a devil. The prosecutor wasn't simply
after someone charged with a brutal beating. He was after someone
who was carrying a burden beyond all human capacity.

That had been hard for me to see. I'd had no trouble seeing how
Billings was being used, or defendants in other trials, but Washington was vastly more powerful, and I'd blinded myself to the fact

that, just as people don't have to be utterly blameless, they don't have to be utterly helpless to become scapegoats. How much easier on our consciences when they aren't!

5:00: The press had filled the first two rows. Several tiers of spectators were standing in the back of the room. The bailiff was monitoring the aisle, keeping it clear. The dignitaries' seats were filled with the DA's senior staff. Everyone was talking. Voices roared.

Washington and the defender were back. Washington talked and joked with friends in the audience. He was loud. His speech was slurred. Suddenly he veered around and called out to a senior DA, "Gray, I forgive you for 1968" (when Washington had been on trial and Gray had been his prosecutor). He rushed over to where Gray was sitting, tweaked Gray's cheek and tried to shake Gray's hand, but Gray remained stiff, looking the other way.

5:15: The judge was still in his office. Every other day he'd adjourned at five. Reporters were saying that he was keeping the jurors longer that day because he wanted to break the deadlock. The noise mounted.

5:40: The judge came out of his office and sat at his desk. He told the bailiff to call the jury down to the courtroom. He looked at his hands as he spoke. He was mumbling.

The bailiff buzzed the jury room. He opened the side door. I heard the metallic echo of footsteps on the stairs.

The jurors filed in. Some took their seats, but then there was confusion over by the door. The reporter from KXAF told me he thought the two holdouts had just given in. He said he overheard something the foreman said to the judge.

The judge sent the jury back upstairs. Take another vote, he said. The defender objected. Washington yelled, "For god's sake, let these people go home!"

5:50: The bailiff's buzzer sounded. The bailiff jumped up. He rushed upstairs to the jury room and came back down with a message in his hand. He rushed into the judge's office with four lawyers on his heels.

The prosecutor came out of the judge's office. Smiling at one of the senior DA's, he whispered, "Verdict." I could read his lips.

5:55: The jurors filed back into the courtroom. Juror number four was smiling. I wanted to call out to her that jurors are only supposed to smile when there's been an acquittal.

The judge came out of his office. Seated, he was a black silhouette against the flag. On either side of him was a bailiff. Looking through the glass in the rear doors, I could see three more bailiffs in the vestibule outside.

5:57: The judge asked the jury if it had reached a verdict. The foreman said yes.

Washington and the defender stood.

The foreman handed the judge a sealed envelope. The judge handed the envelope to the clerk. The clerk ripped it open and began reading out loud with a trembling voice: "On the first count," the gun charges, "we the jury find the defendant, Marvin Washington, guilty," as everyone expected. On the next count, the assault, "we, the jury, find the defendant Marvin Washington . . . Not Guilty."

Not guilty? Not guilty! The whisper rolled through the courtroom like a huge wave. The judge was ashen.

"Is this a unanimous verdict?" the judge asked the foreman. His voice was shaking.

"Yes," the foreman replied.

Washington was frozen, but then he sprang up and yelled to his comrades, "Cheer for the jury!" He waved his arms, and jurors let their smiles break through as half the audience clapped and cheered.

"Is this a unanimous verdict?" the judge asked again.

"Yes," the foreman replied.

There was more cheering and clapping.

The prosecutor buried his face in his hands.

11

The People v. Nicholas David Black

"They always say it isn't their fault, that it's because they're black—you know, racism." We were in the spectators' section, the old woman and I, and Nick was at the lawyers' table, the set mouth and dull cast to his eyes concealing whatever he was feeling.

"I don't know. He doesn't look crazy to me." The old woman didn't tell me her name, only that she was the victim's grandmother. She was in the row ahead of me, sideways on the edge of her chair, and as she pulled the eyeglasses from her face, leaving them to dangle below her neck from a thin black cord, her eyes searched mine.

Tom would have been twenty-four, she said. He'd worked in a nursery, he'd loved plants and flowers, he'd had friends of all races. Her daughter, Tom's mother, wouldn't come to the trial. She told the old woman not to come either. What good would it do? The words stopped, but the old woman's eyes remained on mine. She nodded, acknowledging what we both knew. Her loss was unbearable. I think she believed Nick would somehow carry her grief away with him if he went to prison. I think she believed that if Nick was punished she'd be whole again.

The side door swung open, and the old woman turned to watch the jurors filing into the courtroom. They were all white—men and

women who lived modestly in the suburbs as she did. She smiled
sadly.

There were other spectators. A law student sat next to me. And a
man from the DA's staff was in the back row near the door, his left
foot propped up on his right knee. And an old man from a court-
watching group was across the aisle. There was a tall, lean man with
an Afro who flowed into the contours of his chair and, a few seats
away, a dark-skinned woman who sat with her hands in her lap
looking directly at Nick. The black man was Nick's friend, and the
black woman was Nick's aunt. I'd met them both. They were active
in Nick's defense. Nick was luckier than most defendants, having
people working for him, raising money and helping the lawyers.
He'd been a staunch union member. He had a lot of friends. His
friends said if it hadn't been for Nick's involvement in the union,
this terrible tragedy mightn't have happened.

It was going to be a long trial. The judge had already warned the
jurors about that. He'd told them there were going to be forty witnesses, maybe more, and because Nick was pleading insanity, the
trial was going to be held in two stages. It was going to be two
separate trials. First the jury was going to decide what crime Nick
was guilty of. Nick admitted to the killing. The jury wouldn't have
to decide that. But had he committed first or second degree murder,
or manslaughter? The prosecutor had told the jury that this was cold
blooded murder, pure and simple. But I'd talked to the defender and
I knew that when it was his turn to make his opening argument to
the jury, he was going to say there were two victims here. He was
going to say Nick was a victim too. Nick couldn't be guilty of, say,
first degree murder because he was acutely paranoid at the time of
the shooting, too ill to act with careful thought or premeditation. It
was going to be a diminished capacity defense.

After deciding between murder and manslaughter in part one of
the trial, the jury would then decide whether or not Nick had been
sane, whether he understood what he was doing when he shot
Thomas White or whether he knew it was wrong. The jury could
find Nick guilty of some charge in part one of the trial and then turn
around and find him not guilty by reason of insanity in part two.

Nick's two lawyers were confident. They were sure their case was
strong. They were both in their early thirties. The defender was a
slight man who twitched and fidgeted under the weight of a dark

flannel suit. His associate was more relaxed. Before the trial the lawyers told me they were banking on a manslaughter conviction, which meant a relatively short stay in prison. They said they planned to withdraw the insanity plea, to skip part two of the trial, unless something went wrong and the jury came out with a murder conviction in part one. They believed going to prison for a short while was preferable to being sent indefinitely to the state hospital, which was what would happen if Nick were found insane. They said Nick himself knew about the state hospital. After his arrest, he'd been sent there, and psychiatrists had had him shackled to a bed and then had denied him beneficial drugs so they could observe him in his distraught state.

It was one of those balmy late winter days. I took off my sweater. As I arranged it over the back of the seat, I smiled at the law student next to me who told me he was attending the trial because he was especially interested in the insanity defense. He said he'd learned about the case through one of the local alternative weeklies, which was how I'd learned about the case too, although it had been the political issues that had lured me to the trial. The defense was charging that International Machine Company, where Nick worked, locked minority employees into low paying jobs by excluding them from training programs. The defense was claiming that workers who protested this treatment were harassed, that it was harassment that had pushed Nick over the edge, making him crazy enough to go out and kill. The defense was saying that International Machine Company, one of the largest companies in the country, was responsible for Tom White's death, that it isn't necessarily the person who fires the gun who's responsible.

I was eager to hear the question of social responsibility raised in a courtroom for a change.

THE PROSECUTION

"Mrs. Catherine Alverado, is that correct?"
"Yes."
"On October 21st last year at approximately five thirty in the afternoon were you parked westbound on Banyon near Croft with Susan Mendoza and Diane Aguilar?"
"Yes, I was."

"Were you parked at the time in front of the Taco Stand?"

"Yes." She and her friends were sitting in her car, eating tacos and drinking lemonade through straws, joking and kidding around. Not too far in the distance the hills stood up over the tops of stores, grass still brown from the summer drought, almost purple in the fading light, while along Banyon Street cars whooshed by — a sleek yellow LTD, a white and green tow truck, a gray Toyota. The three women didn't notice the light on the corner turning red, or the cars stopping, or the humming, or the throbbing, although Diane Aguilar did stop eating long enough to fan exhaust fumes away with her hand.

It wasn't until the crash that Catherine Alverado looked out the car window, not a big crash, but loud enough to hear. A blue Maverick with a white top hit a green Triumph from behind, knocking off the tail light. Alverado saw the drivers get out of their cars, and "the man from the green car was asking for something, and the man from the blue car said, 'You're not getting anything from me.' Then the man from the green car backed off a little bit, and he threw his hands out, and he says, 'I have to get something because you dented my car,' and he walked back to his car."

Susan Mendoza gulped down the last of her lemonade and sat forward to see, and Diane Aguilar crumpled up her napkin and dropped it on the floor and leaned over across the dash. The first man was back in his Triumph, reaching into the glove compartment for a pencil and paper. The other man was back inside his car, reaching down for something also. "And then the defendant got out of his car and walked over to the man in the green car who was still sitting in his car. He pulled out a gun and he shot him three times in the head for no reason."

He shot him three times in the head for no reason. No reason. Catherine Alverado pressed her hand to her mouth. She wanted to look away, but she couldn't. She sat and stared, and her friends didn't make a sound.

"The defendant just went back to his car, like nothing happened. He got into his car and backed up and looked over at all of us and just pulled out in the left hand lane and drove away down the street."

"At that time did you go to Thomas White's car, the green Triumph?"

"Yes, I did."

"And what did you observe when you got there?"

"He was laying, he was leaning over toward the passenger side. He had blood on his head, and he also had a pencil in his hand still."

Susan Mendoza testified too, telling almost the same story, and Diane Aguilar, and Ron Jackson and Earl Richmond who had been across on the other side of Banyon Street having a conversation, and Joseph Whitcomb, a security guard, who had been having a hamburger at the burger place behind the Taco Stand. Even though there was so much repetition, I didn't lose interest. This was a story you needed told and retold.

At the recess I stood in the hallway with the law student and another reporter, discussing the trial. The reporter was a young man who had arrived just as the testimony had begun. He and I were the only reporters covering the trial.

The law student said that everyone's story was so similar it would be the small details that would make the difference. He gave as an example Mendoza saying she saw Nick holding the gun down by his side as he walked to the victim's car. That made it look like Nick was trying to conceal the weapon. A good lawyer could make a lot out of that little detail, using it to show that Nick premeditated the killing, that he not only knew what he was doing but that he also knew it was wrong.

Joseph Whitcomb, the security guard, had said Nick looked angry. The law student talked about that too, saying Whitcomb made it sound like Nick had some motive, like the killing wasn't entirely senseless as Alverado said.

But the reporter reminded him that during cross examination Whitcomb admitted that he'd been too far away to hear or see the expression on Nick's face. He said he made his judgment by observing how Nick moved his body. None of the other witnesses thought Nick looked angry. Disinterested, not willing to be bothered, in a hurry to be somewhere maybe, something like that, was how Ron Jackson said he thought Nick looked, but not angry.

Even if Nick had been angry, the reporter went on, that wouldn't necessarily support the prosecution. Maybe Nick killed Tom White because he was angry at someone else. That would support the defense's claim that he wasn't in his right mind. The reporter said he thought if the prosecutor was going to show a motive, he'd have to prove Nick knew Tom White before the accident.

The law student smiled and said if he were the prosecutor he'd say Nick killed the young man to keep him from reporting the accident to his insurance company.

"You think the jury would believe he'd kill a man so he wouldn't have to pay for breaking a tail light?" the reporter asked in disbelief.

The law student nodded.

We had all those details to discuss, and we talked them over for quite some time, although it was the law student and the reporter really who did most of the talking. I told the law student I wasn't convinced that the facts of the case mattered very much. I didn't think juries' decisions were that rational. Too much happened at trials to obscure the issues.

Without so much as a shiver, Nick got into his car. As he drove off, pulling into the left lane slowly, never exceeding the speed limit, a woman who had just walked past the Taco Stand thought to jot down the license number. When minutes later a man rushed out into the traffic to hail down a police car coming from the other direction—it must have passed Nick's car right by—the woman rushed out too with her precious slip of paper.

So it was that Officers Elvis Simon and Daniel Dickson heard the news over their two way radio on their way to City Hall. "That's us," Officer Simon said and Officer Dickson turned the large van left onto Carver, and then left again onto 38th, past little stucco houses with tidy green lawns, back toward the shopping center. At Banyon, Officer Dickson made another left, away from the shopping center now, driving on, not too slowly, but not too fast, so he and his partner could check up and down the cross streets. They passed 37th and 36th, and a dingy liquor store, and an empty laundromat, and empty lots, and men and women hurrying home from work, and the steady stream of oncoming traffic.

"As we approached 34th Avenue, I saw a vehicle that appeared to match the description of the suspect vehicle," Officer Simon told the jury. He was trying to sound matter of fact, but if you listened hard, you could catch the slight tremor in his voice, and the breathlessness. "The driver looked right at us and then he made a left turn so he was traveling eastbound on Banyon, back toward the scene of the shooting. I made a U-turn, and I activated my red light and siren, and I started to follow the vehicle which sped up, and we broadcast on the radio our location and what was happening."

Officer Simon shuddered.

Sirens screeched, cars flew to the scene. Officer Dickson and Officer Simon were joined by Officer Fredericks and Officer Williams, and Officer Alexander on his motorcycle, all of whom had abandoned their regular beats, while Officer Barstow waited in his marked car at the corner of Croft and Banyon, listening to the chase drawing near. Officer Barstow planned to ram into the side of the suspect vehicle as it sped by, but then he had second thoughts because he knew the suspect was armed and he didn't want to be in the line of fire. The light turned red. The suspect vehicle stopped dead in the left hand lane behind a line of traffic. Officer Barstow joined the other police cars massed thirty feet or so behind. As the men got out of their cars, Officer Alexander flew past them on his motorcycle, pulling up alongside the blue and white car with his gun drawn, calling out something like, "Halt!" or "Stop and put your hands on the wheel!" or "Hold it, don't move!" — something like that. Afterwards no one could remember precisely what it was. The person in the vehicle looked at Officer Alexander then ducked forward near the steering wheel and came back up with his right hand and fired the pistol. He missed. The officer immediately returned the fire, but his motorcycle started to fall over and he momentarily lost his balance.

Hearing the shots, seeing Officer Alexander fall, the other officers took their positions, crouching behind the doors of their cars, rushing out in the open and then back for cover. Simon got off two shots; Barstow got off four; Williams got off three; and Officer Fredericks blasted his shotgun four times which took out the rear window of the suspect's car. There was a lull, and the suspect ducked down, and everyone stopped shooting. It was so still you could hear the cross traffic in the distance and the throbbing of idling cars.

Officer Fredericks advanced toward the car. The light turned green, the Maverick pulled ahead, and a barrage of shots whizzed after the suspect car. Officer Simon ran to see if Officer Alexander was hurt. Officer Dickson ran to the van to call for an ambulance. The other three officers took off after the Maverick which had zoomed through the light up near the fried chicken stand and crashed into the side of a light blue Pinto, then skidded onto the island and over into the wrong left turn lane.

Officer Williams saw the suspect running down the dividing island. In the distance a billboard announced ROYAL GATE GOES GREAT. He pulled out his shotgun and ran off after the suspect shouting for him to halt. Someone, a civilian standing near the empty lot, shouted, "Stop or he'll shoot you!" and the suspect stopped short right there as if someone had taken away his legs.

It was Officer Williams who put on the handcuffs and cut off the suspect's shirt and saw he'd been shot in the back and in the neck and in the hand. It was Officer Barstow who called the ambulance.

By then police officers were all around. Some of them began collecting evidence, tiny fragments, precious relics, which they carefully dropped into paper bags to store until the trial. They collected shell casings from the suspect's car and pieces of tail light and bloodstained upholstery from the victim's. Later they collected the bullets from the victim's body, and the suspect's brown levi pants and his brown belt and a pair of brown scuffed boots and a book of matches and a package of Kool cigarettes and a box of bullets and one hundred twenty-seven dollars from his pockets.

One at a time these bits and pieces were shown to the jury, each an offering painstakingly removed from its container, each held up to the silvery shimmering light, while the judge officiated and lawyers asked questions and witnesses answered in an antiphonal chant. One at a time these bits and pieces were returned to their packages and entrusted to the clerk who gave each one a special mark.

At the recess I listened to the law student and the reporter analyzing the testimony, searching for clues, for snatches of what was to come.

The law student said the prosecutor would argue that Nick had been on the attack, since he'd fired the first shot.

But the reporter said the defender would argue that Nick had been on the defensive since it was Officer Alexander who first drew a gun.

The law student said the prosecutor would argue that in trying to run away, even after he was surrounded, Nick showed he knew he had committed a terrible crime.

But the reporter said it was clear to him that Nick had to be out of his mind to put himself in such danger.

The law student said that when Nick made the left turn and drove away from the police van, he showed that he knew well what he had done and that it was wrong.

But the reporter asked why ten minutes after the shooting Nick would still be in the area, why he wouldn't be on some freeway or, with $127 in his pocket, at the airport, if he were in his right mind.

Everyone knew Nick's state of mind was critically important — that was what the trial was supposed to be about — but I told the reporter and the law student I didn't see how the jury could make any decision about Nick's thoughts or notions on the basis of the shreds of evidence they had so far. They were reducing a complex human being to a set of scientific indicators. Making everything sound so rational and scientific was masking what was really going on.

THE DEFENSE

"The first day he was in court I waved, but he didn't pay me no mind. He was in his pajamas, and he didn't have his hair combed. But look at him now. He's coming to himself." Nick's aunt was talking to me. She was staring at Nick who was sitting at the lawyers' table in a fresh knit shirt. She sounded far away, but she was smiling, and there was a softness about her that was attractive.

"I've known him since he was a boy," she told me. "There wasn't no malice in him. No, it had to be because he was under the strain of a nervous breakdown. They kept pulling him down until he went into this." She passed her hands over the folds of skin along her neck.

She told me Nick's father had struggled to raise seven children. He'd raised a girl to be a school teacher, a boy to go to college. "His father worked till the day he died. There wasn't any of them on welfare," she said.

A young woman in levis and a V-neck sweater, a member of the law collective that was representing Nick, stooped down to whisper something to his aunt. I couldn't hear what she was saying, but I was sure it concerned the defense which was scheduled to begin that morning. She went to the lawyers' table where she handed the lawyers some papers. She smiled warmly at Nick who returned the smile.

Nick had been a member of a workers' antidiscrimination committee which had engaged the law collective the year before to sue

International Machine for civil rights violations, so he'd known the woman and the lawyers for some time. He wasn't going to testify in his own behalf (everyone said he wasn't well enough for that) but as he sat in the courtroom listening to others tell his story for him, he'd know friends were close by.

Nick looked behind him over his shoulder. He grinned at his aunt. But when the judge came, and then the jury, his face sobered. In their presence he hid his feelings, just as they did in his presence, just as Frank Beecher did minutes later, the tall wiry man with sandy hair and soft blue eyes who took the stand as the first witness for the defense.

"Mr. Beecher, where are you employed?"

"International Machine Company."

"What is your position there?"

"Factory superintendent."

"What is that? What does that job entail?"

"I'm in charge of the factory area with general foremen under me and approximately five hundred hourly employees."

"And do you know the defendant in this case, Nicholas Black?"

"Yes."

"Referring to last October 21st, did you see Mr. Black?"

"Yes."

"Will you tell us what happened?"

"Yes." Beecher craned his neck forward and began speaking so slowly and deliberately it was as if he didn't want to testify. "It was about eight in the morning, just outside my office. I said good morning to him, and he just walked past me."

"Did you see him later on?"

"Yes, a few minutes later, as I was walking down through the shop in the area where he formerly worked. His foreman told me that Nick had come into the department, picked up his tool box and left. When the foreman asked him was he going to go to work, he said, 'No, I'm not working today.' "

"Was it unusual for him to leave with his tool box?"

"Well, normally they won't be taking their tool box with them unless they've been discharged or quit, and then they have to go through a procedure, having the tool box checked to get it outside the plant." Beecher said he went out to the main gate to see if Nick had left and, finding he hadn't, he went back inside to labor relations where no one had seen him either. Beecher said he returned to the main gate and waited for about ten minutes, out in back of the plant, down the street from a row of rundown houses, back by the guard station where he chatted with Jerry Miller, the uniformed guard. "I decided that I'd better start looking for Nick and finding out where he was and what he was doing." Inside the corrugated building, he looked up and down the rows where workers were bent over screeching machines. He was so used to the noise he barely noticed it. Nor did he notice the dust dancing beneath fluorescent lights strung ten feet below crisscrossing steel rafters.

"I couldn't find Nick, and so I decided to get ahold of the chief shop steward, Whitney Harris. When I found Whitney I asked him if he'd seen Nick, and he said, 'Yeah, he's running a machine over there in department thirty-seven,' which is in another building across the street from where he normally works," Beecher said. Together he and Harris went to find Nick, the willowy white man and the squat black man, two old timers. They talked as they went, raising their voices over the roar of passing trucks. They found Nick where Harris had said he'd be, running a machine. "It appeared he was trying to stone the side of some drill collets, but there's no need to ever do that. It's nonsense work. It doesn't make any sense." Beecher went over to Nick to ask what he was doing. "He just picked up the drill, put everything in his tool box and locked it up. He stood there for a moment or two, and then he picked up his tool box and started walking. He wandered rather aimlessly through the plant, up one aisle, down the other, through several departments, and he finally stopped outside of department fifteen and stood there. I asked him was he going to work or was he going to leave the premises. He walked down to his department, went to his normally assigned machine and started it up, running the machine probably for about five minutes without any piece parts in it."

Beecher said he and Harris talked it over. They agreed something was wrong. Harris had seen Nick earlier with a funny look, almost like he was in a trance, working and smiling and laughing so loud that at first everyone thought someone else was at the machine with him, and now the two men watched him behind a machine that was just oscillating back and forth. They watched him standing there with a faraway look in his eyes, and they listened to the beating of the machine.

"I asked Nick to go to the medical department so we could have him checked. He didn't respond at all. I then asked Whitney Harris if he would talk to Nick, which he did." The black man put his hand on Nick's shoulder and talked to him some, and Nick went to medical where they sat Nick down, and the nurse questioned him, and he couldn't remember his middle initial. She asked him who his foreman was. He didn't know. Then she took him into the examining room. Beecher could see Nick standing in front of the long full-length mirror, going through all kinds of motions with his hands, bowing, swinging his arms around, talking to himself in front of the mirror.

"The nurse came out and said that she had taken his blood pressure, and I believe she said that his blood pressure was high and that the pupils of his eyes were contracted and nonresponsive, and she felt that he was not capable of working in the shop." Beecher and Harris and some people from labor relations discussed what to do next. At first someone said they should send Nick home, if his family would come and pick him up, since he obviously couldn't drive. But then everyone agreed that it would be better if Andrew Tillingham drove him to County Hospital. He needed to be checked out some more.

"Were you involved in a decision in any way to fire Nick Black last year?"

"Yes, I was."

It was the prosecutor cross examining Beecher. The defender barely had time to sit down before the prosecutor sprang up, jerking his head back to get the hair out of his eyes, facing the witness, asking if he'd been one to decide to fire Nick, smiling faintly as the sound of his own voice shattered the mood the defender had so painstakingly created.

"Can you detail the grounds upon which this defendant was fired?"

"Insubordination."

"Prior to the actual firing of this defendant, had there been instances of insubordination?"

"Yes."

"Approximately how many, if you recall?"

"Three or four."

"Had the defendant been given a final warning?"

"Yes."

"Do you know if after the giving of that final warning he was again insubordinate on any occasion?"

"Yes."

"And do you recall the details of that incident?"

"Somewhat. He was questioned by his foreman as to an aspect of his job, and he refused to talk to his foreman."

"So that when the defendant did not talk to certain people, certain people in positions of supervision over him on October 21st, that was not the first time that he had been unresponsive to his supervisors?"

"That's right."

"And after Andrew Tillingham took the defendant to the hospital, did you see the defendant later that day?"

"Yes."

"And where was that? Where did you see him?"

"In front of the plant."

"Do you remember what time it was?"

"About four o'clock."

"How did he appear to you?"

"He appeared to be going toward his car, which I would assume was parked in the parking lot."

"Was there anything you noticed when you saw the defendant that afternoon, anything you noticed about his condition that stuck out in your mind?"

"No, not particularly."

"Is it correct that after he was fired earlier in the year, that as a result of union pressure he was reinstated?"

"As a result of a third step grievance he was reinstated, yes."

"Are you familiar with a work evaluation that was made of Mr. Black in the summer of last year?"

"Yes, I am. It said that he was not capable of performing the job he was on at that point in time. He was operating turret lathes, and he was not capable of operating them at a satisfactory level . . ."

"You're talking about a skill level?"

"Yes."

Unskilled. Rude. Earlier, when Beecher was answering the defender's questions, I was sure he was saying Nick wasn't normal, wasn't well, wasn't himself. And the way he sat so straight, the way he clutched at the arms of the chair, made me think he was worried that the company *had* been too hard on Nick, that it *had* driven him insane. It made me think that for the moment at least Frank Beecher was uncomfortable in his managerial role.

But then, facing the prosecutor, Beecher looked different. I was sure I saw him relax. When the prosecutor asked him if Nick had been unresponsive to his supervisors before the day of the shooting, I was sure I heard Beecher sigh with relief as he answered his own question, yes. Yes, he's unskilled, yes. Yes, he's rude, yes. Yes, he deserves it, yes.

When the judge excused him, Beecher walked briskly out of the courtroom avoiding the defender's eyes.

The reporter leaned across me and whispered to the law student that Beecher's description of Nick's strange behavior just the morning before the killing made the defense case terribly strong, especially when the prosecutor had shown that Beecher wasn't Nick's ally.

The law student reminded the reporter that Beecher hadn't seen anything peculiar about Nick when he ran into him later at four.

The reporter said he thought the earlier testimony overcame that. The four o'clock encounter had been so brief, and from such a distance.

The law student reminded the reporter that the prosecutor was going to argue that, up close or far away, Beecher had been talking about a man who was lazy and rude, not crazy. If it hadn't been for union pressure, Nick would have been fired.

I agreed with the law student. I thought that was precisely what the prosecutor would say. He would dig up whatever he could to make Nick look bad. He was just biding his time.

"Your name is Whitney Harris?"

"Yes."

"Mr. Harris, by whom are you employed?"

"International Machine Company."

"How long have you been employed there?"

"Oh, approximately eight years."

"And what kind of work do you do?"

"I'm a machinist."

"Are you a member of the union?"

"Yes, I am. I'm the union representative through the first two steps of the grievance procedure. I'm the chief steward."

"Is there any other union official who is above you who actually works at International?"

"No, there's not."

When Whitney Harris took the stand as a defense witness, he didn't wait for the bailiff to help him. As soon as the defender called out his name, he came down the aisle to be sworn in, he sat in the witness chair, and before the bailiff had time to reach over, he adjusted the microphone himself. He glanced at the jury. He looked down on Nick like a father looking at his son, and when he listed his credentials, he seemed to be taking his self importance and holding it out in his hands, saying to Nick, "Here, you take it all. It's bound to help. I don't want them taking you away."

He explained to the jury that he first met Nick when Nick came to him because he wanted his foreman off his back. Other black workers had had trouble with the same foreman too, and he told Nick the proper course would be through the grievance procedure. He hadn't wanted Nick to do anything to jeopardize his job.

He said Nick was elected shop steward by the employees in three departments. Nick was an important member of the union elections committee too and often came to meetings at Harris' home.

Harris and Nick became close, the older man and the fatherless son. Nick got involved with other workers who complained of discrimination. He joined their antidiscrimination committee, and during breaks and after work he went around and spoke to the workers.

When the company suspended Nick, the union investigated and found there was no basis for the suspension and Nick returned to work. Everything seemed okay until a week or two later when the company moved Nick to a new department which meant he had to give up the shop steward job. "Nick told me he felt it was unfair that he was moved because he had did nothing, all he wanted to do was work, and to my knowledge that's all he did," Whitney Harris said, brushing his cheek with the back of his hand.

"You have been union representative in how many grievances, Mr. Harris?"

"I don't know, somewhere between eight hundred and thirteen hundred."

"Of those eight hundred to thirteen hundred grievances, how many of those involved either firing or suspension?"

"I would say approximately fifteen percent."

"And, of that number, of the fifteen percent, how many of those individuals were eventually reinstated as a result of union activity?"

"Approximately fourteen percent."

"So almost all of them were reinstated?"

"Yes, well give or take . . ."

The prosecutor was smiling.

After Whitney Harris left the courtroom, Lloyd Carpenter took the stand. He identified himself as Nick's coworker and as a member of the antidiscrimination committee. He was a tall, lithe man with light brown skin, somewhat older than Nick. He wove his fingers together and made circles with his thumbs.

He explained that the antidiscrimination committee was trying to stop some of the systematic discrimination at International. He said the committee was going to federal court in the hopes of winning concessions. He himself had been harassed by management when, some time back, the police arrested him and terrorized his wife who was six months pregnant. Carpenter said they released him because he hadn't done anything wrong and later a supervisor at work indicated that the company had been behind the arrest.

"I met Nick, I think it was a year and a half ago, on the strike line, the last strike we had at International," Carpenter told the jury. "I looked at him and I liked him. He was like myself, a determined, ambitious young man. Mr. Whitney Harris mobilized a vehicle to elect some workers at International to become officers of the local. Nick was at all of the meetings, a very concerned individual."

Carpenter said the stewardship was the most important thing that had ever happened to Nick, and he said Nick changed after the company transferred him to a different department. He acted disturbed. "Normally he was a very quiet person, but then he kept repeating himself. Like, he took over meetings. He was loud. He acted strange. He kept repeating himself. Nobody else could hardly say anything. He kept repeating he was a good worker, he was being harassed." Carpenter said Nick didn't look right either. "He looked strange, like . . ." Carpenter stood. "He just . . ." Carpenter put up his hands. "He just looked nervous." Carpenter sat down.

★   ★   ★

"Each of these things, his being fired, his losing his shop steward-ship, his evaluation of being below acceptable skill level—he was right to be angry about all these things, is that right?" the prosecutor asked.

"Well, concerned. I don't know if angry is the right word to use," Carpenter replied.

"In your opinion was he being persecuted?"

"Oh, yes."

"He was?"

"Right. I think so."

"Do you feel that you are persecuted by International Machine Company?"

"I can prove it to you, document it."

"You feel that International is out to get you, is that correct?"

"Out to get me?"

"Do you feel that International is persecuting you?"

"Yes, in a way, yes."

"Of course he's trying to make them look dumb. That's his job," the law student was whispering to the reporter.

The reporter was shaking his head. "He's making the charge of racism sound frivolous. He's pandering to the white jury." He said that even if the jurors weren't prejudiced there was too much they couldn't understand about Nick's experiences because their back-grounds were so different.

The law student said he didn't think it was essential for the jury to understand Nick's background. Carpenter and Harris were raising real doubt about Nick's mental capacity, and that was what the trial was about.

I said I didn't agree. I didn't think that was what the trial was about. I thought the trial was a struggle between two lawyers to define Nick's face. Nick was there before the jury not saying a word, wearing a blank expression. I said I thought the defender was trying to portray Nick as a victim and the prosecutor was trying to portray him as an aggressor. Winning that struggle was what the trial was about.

★   ★   ★

Andrew Tillingham, the personnel supervisor at International, took
Nick to County Hospital, out onto the freeway, along the bay, up
over the streets toward the hills where the Mormon temple sits close
to the sun. He passed by the old marble hospital behind the stately
pines, driving for several blocks to the twenty-five-cent parking lot
in front of the new building. Along the way, Nick asked Tillingham
for a cigarette, which Tillingham didn't have, but for most of the
ride Nick was quiet, unusually quiet Tillingham thought. Inside the
emergency entrance, Nick approached a man for a cigarette and
Tillingham talked to the receptionist. She was a woman in white
behind a twenty-foot counter, asking questions above talking and
typing and people coming and going and doors swinging open and
shut and the TV saying if you went to Hunter's View College you
would learn a skill and earn money at the same time.

The receptionist called Nick over. She asked him his name, where
he worked, did he want to see a doctor. Nick said he didn't know
why he was there, but if the company wanted him to see a doctor he
would see one. She looked at Tillingham and she said, "Well, why
do you want him to see a doctor? There doesn't seem to be anything
wrong with him." Tillingham explained that Nick had been acting
strange, the company insisted on him seeing a doctor. He told her
International would pay the bill.

The receptionist said okay. Tillingham left. Nick waited in an
examining room until Nurse Schumacher came in and asked him to
sit on the gurney and undress for the doctor. Nurse Schumacher was
in her twenties. She was tall. She wore her honey colored hair in a
bun. When Nick told her that he had passed out at work, that he felt
tired, she asked him whether he hit his head or whether he had a
history of seizures or diabetes.

Mostly Nick was quiet. He did what the nurse asked him to do.
He answered some of her questions, and some he didn't. He told her
he was suing New York State. He handed her a piece of paper,
saying it was very important, that she and the doctor should know
about it. She put it in his folder. Then she went through Nick's
wallet to see if he had money to put in the safe, and she found Nick's
Kaiser card. Knowing that the Kaiser health plan only pays for
medical care performed at Kaiser Hospital, she left Nick in the
examining room to go and arrange for him to be transferred. The

receptionist hadn't told her International was planning to pay Nick's bill.

Meanwhile Dr. Miller, the intern, examined Nick carefully. He talked to him, gave him tests, and found nothing physically wrong, although he was struck by how Nick responded to questions, getting caught up in words, repeating them several times before he could go on, laughing inappropriately. Dr. Miller thought Nick should have a psychiatric evaluation but since there was nothing acutely wrong with him physically, the nurse told him Nick would have to go to Kaiser. Dr. Miller's supervisor, Dr. Shine, checked Nick over briefly too, and he agreed Nick should be seen by a psychiatrist. Learning Nick was insured by Kaiser, Dr. Shine called Kaiser to make an appointment for a psychiatric evaluation. He requested an ambulance, but he was told that unless the patient was acutely ill, Kaiser wouldn't pay for an ambulance.

And so it was that two hours after Andrew Tillingham brought Nick to County Hospital, the nurse or the receptionist, someone behind the counter, called for a taxi. The taxi came. Nick got in. The nurse told the driver to take Nick to Kaiser. The taxi drove off. Nick never kept the appointment.

Nick never kept the appointment. All those medical people saw him, and they saw something was wrong, and they let him slip away, and five hours later. . . . The student, the reporter and I looked at each other, and then we looked at the prosecutor:

"Doctor, did you make a recommendation that Mr. Black be involuntarily committed based on your observation of him?"

"No, I didn't."

"Did you place a psychiatric hold on him?"

"If he hadn't had Kaiser he would have been sent to psychiatric emergency after we knew his lab tests were normal."

"Was he sent in an ambulance?"

"Kaiser wouldn't authorize sending an ambulance. We sent him by taxi. Kaiser has very strict restrictions about how their patients get to them, and we have to follow whatever they tell us on the phone."

"But you *could* have sent him to Kaiser in an ambulance?" It was the judge asking the question. He was staring over the top of his glasses at the doctor, and the prosecutor was staring at the doctor too.

"It wasn't authorized by Kaiser. They wouldn't pay for it."

"Regardless of who pays, couldn't you have sent him in an ambulance?" the prosecutor broke in.

"The county wouldn't pay for it either."

"Let's make it easy," said the judge. "Let's say he was ranting and raving and foaming at the mouth, are you telling me you wouldn't have him sent by ambulance?"

"I would have called the deputies and asked them what they would recommend."

"And in this case you didn't call any deputies?" the prosecutor asked.

"No."

The prosecutor sat down.

The reporter whispered, "Does he have to be frothing at the mouth to be insane?"

The student answered, "The jury will be told he has to be incapable of knowing or understanding the nature and quality of his act or that his act was wrong."

The reporter whispered, "But the judge seems to think that Nick wasn't really sick because he wasn't ranting and raving."

I said, "I thought in this part of the trial Nick's mental capacity was supposed to be the issue, not insanity. Did he have the capacity to premeditate, things like that."

The law student answered, "But this testimony will be used for both parts of the trial. Just the psychiatric testimony will be different. In the insanity phase the psychiatrists will put it in terms of whether Nick understood what he was doing, but in this phase they'll talk about the definitions of murder and manslaughter."

I asked, "What are the definitions?"

"Well, murder is the unlawful killing of a human being with malice aforethought," the law student replied. He was droning, sounding very much like a judge instructing the jury. "Manslaughter is the unlawful killing of a human being without malice aforethought. Malice can be expressed or implied. It is expressed when there is manifested an intention unlawfully to kill someone. It is implied when the killing results from an act having a high degree of probability that it will result in death and when it is done for a base, antisocial purpose. The mental state constituting malice afore-thought does not necessarily require any ill will or hatred of the person killed . . ."

"Whoa! You've lost me," I interrupted the law student who was suddenly grinning.

"Well, don't feel bad. Earlier I heard the judge and defender discussing the meaning of these definitions, and *they* couldn't agree."

Thelma Black was across from Kaiser Hospital, at the bus stop, waiting to go home. She'd been to the doctor. Standing there in the hot noontime sun, she realized how tired she was. She closed her eyes and tilted her head so it was nearly touching her shoulder. Then, with a sigh, she lifted her head and she saw Nicholas, her son, waiting for the bus, just a few feet away. She frowned. She shielded her eyes with her hand. She looked at him. His clothes were wrin-kled up and his hair wasn't combed. She asked, "What's happening, man?"

Nicholas said, "The company sent me to the hospital."

She asked, "What for, man?"

But Nicholas didn't answer except to say, "Don't worry."

The bus came and all the people at the bus stop reached into their purses and pockets and crowded in. Thelma Black got a seat up front, but Nicholas walked right by her as if she weren't there. Sunlight was streaming in through the window, making her knee feel like it was on fire. She shaded it with her purse and dozed off, but then later on, when the bus was half empty and already into East Oakland, she awakened to the sound of Nicholas's voice. She looked back and saw him gazing out the window. He was rocking back and forth, and back and forth, gazing out the window. No one was near him, and he was talking very loud.

As she got off the bus, she said goodbye. She assumed he was going back to the plant. "I saw him again. That must have been around four. He came by my house like he usually does after work. He came by, and I was laying down, so he came in and he says, 'Mom, are you worried?' And I said, 'Not really,' and I asked him what happened, what did they send him to the doctor for. So he kept telling me that I was not to worry, that he was going to be all right, that he was tired of the job, so that was it. Then he told me he was going to leave and go home, and I told him to go home and rest. That's the last I saw him."

"He left at that time?"

"He left at that time."

"How did Nicholas appear to you at that time?"

"At that time, well, the same, you know, he was just moving and kind of stretching, you know, and very strange."

"Very strange?"

"Very strange. He was just not Nicholas."

"Mrs. Black, you said Nick was acting very strange. Did you call the police?" the prosecutor asked.

"Did I call the police? No."

"Did you call the doctor?"

"No. Did I call the doctor? No." It was cross examination. Thelma Black responded to the cold questions slowly, with caution.

"During the time Nick was on the bus, did the bus driver, to your knowledge, call anybody, police officers, doctors, anybody?"

"Not to my knowledge."

"Did you talk to Nick after he was fired from his job?"

"Yes. He told me what happened."

"And was he angry about that?"

"I would say upset. I wouldn't say he was angry. I don't know."

"Did you notice during the last year any change in Nick's political viewpoints?" the prosecutor asked.

"I don't understand the question," Mrs. Black replied.

"Did Nick seem to become, during that time, more concerned with, what, working class versus management relations, things like that?"

"Oh, yes." Mrs. Black shrugged as if to say, of course he did.

"Did Nick talk to you about conditions at International?"

"Yes, he did."

"Did he talk to you about the antidiscrimination committee?"

"Yes, he did."

"Did he talk to you when he was transferred from one job to another and lost the job of being shop steward?"

"Yes, he did."

"Was he angry about that?"

"I will say upset. Angry? Yes, very much." Thelma Black

shrugged again. What man in his position wouldn't be angry, she seemed to say.

"Did Nick also take an interest in religion?"

"Take an interest in religion?"

"Yes, during that time."

"Not to my knowledge." Mrs. Black looked puzzled.

"Nick wasn't connected with the Black Muslims?"

"Was not connected with the Black Muslims? Not at this time to my knowledge . . . He was. He *had* been, if that's what you're asking me," Thelma Black said, and when the prosecutor said he had no further questions, she stepped down from the stand, she crossed the bar, and she came slowly down the aisle, a tiny woman with jet black hair and smooth brown skin.

She passed by her husband's sister in the spectators' section, and by her son's friend. Her hands were fists.

"Now, Dr. Dudley, were any of the statements that the defendant made to you medically significant?" the defender asked.

"Yes," Dr. Dudley replied.

"And what are the statements that he made to you that you felt were of medical significance?"

"He indicated . . ."

"Wait. What do you mean by medically significant?" the judge interrupted. He was peering at Dr. Dudley, a black man somewhere in his fifties who was wearing a knit suit that seemed terribly heavy for such a warm day.

"By medically significant, I was narrowing it down to my primary interest in the field of psychiatry," Dr. Dudley explained. "Whether the statements were of psychiatric significance to me."

"Based on what he told you, you reached an opinion at some point, or made a diagnosis, is that correct?" the judge asked.

"Yes, your honor. The diagnosis was made upon the information obtained from the interview, yes, your honor," Dr. Dudley replied.

"Proceed, Mr. Defender," the judge said, still peering at Dr. Dudley.

In the seat next to mine the reporter tugged at the collar of his jacket. On my other side the law student was slumped on his spine. Behind me someone coughed, and in the jury box several jurors shifted in their chairs. The witness was rummaging through his attaché case, sifting through a stack of notes. He was a psychiatrist the court had appointed to evaluate Nick's behavior four months earlier, two months after the shooting. He seemed oddly nervous, considering he'd testified as an expert many times before.

A jailkeeper had testified before Dr. Dudley about Nick's behavior a week after the shooting when Nick was transferred from the county hospital to the courthouse jail. The jailkeeper said Nick stuffed a bedsheet down the toilet and later set fire to his cell. His behavior was so bizarre that the jail officials sent him to the state hospital for the criminally insane. The jailkeeper's testimony fit in nicely with all the rest, a sheriff's man agreeing that Nick wasn't in his right mind. But now, as Dr. Dudley testified, the pace slowed. It was still part one of the trial, but having the psychiatrist on the stand made it feel like the beginning of part two.

"Which of the statements the defendant made to you did you consider significant in terms of reaching your diagnosis?" the defender asked Dr. Dudley again.

"Well, there were several statements," the doctor replied. "And predominantly they were statements that were in the area of projecting, such as he was hearing voices, and the voices were making fun of him. The other set of things that were going on consisted of a system of false beliefs, what I call a delusional system, and he considered himself associated with the devil. He was afraid of the devil being after him. He also had a set of delusions that some people were out to put a contract on him. At times the contract seems to have emanated from people associated with International Machine and other times with other people." Dr. Dudley said Nick had heard voices that weren't validated by anyone else's hearing ability. He said Nick hadn't known where the voices were coming from. He was reading his notes as he testified, so his words were directed down toward his lap and were difficult to understand. He also paused a lot between sentences, which made it seem that he hadn't looked at his notes for some time.

"And what were the voices saying to him?" the defender asked.

"Let's see. One set of voices was making fun of him. We didn't go into too much detail about the voices because after getting a picture of auditory hallucinations, we could have stayed there for hours getting the details about them."

"You just used the term auditory hallucination. What does that term mean to you? Can you explain that in lay language?"

"Yes. By auditory hallucination we mean the person is at that time experiencing a distortion of his perception, that he is capable of actually hearing voices when no one else is around. Frequently these may be of a persecutory nature. Sometimes they are pretty close to what one would ordinarily have in the so-called normal consciousness, all the way to the..."

"Boy, this man talks in paragraphs, not sentences," the reporter leaned over and whispered.

"Really!" The law student grinned.

I smiled too, although I wasn't amused. We'd talked earlier about how important Dr. Dudley's testimony was to the defense. He was supposed to put a name to the peculiar behavior everyone else had been describing. He was supposed to make it official that Nick had been ill. But instead he was creating confusion. He was talking about hallucinations without describing them so people could understand, so they could feel what Nick must have felt. How horrible it must be to hear voices talking to you from inside your own head. They must echo. They must make you feel like running away from yourself. They must make you think your body is occupied by supernatural beings. They must make you think all sorts of terrifying things which the doctor didn't describe. Dr. Dudley didn't seem to realize that most people don't know what hallucinations are.

I was sorry Nick wasn't on the stand himself. I wanted to hear *him* say what it had been like. I remembered one defendant testifying about being shot in the back by a policeman. He'd said immediately after he'd felt like he was floating. His description had been so vivid, I'd felt like *I* was being shot. But Nick was reliant on others to convey his thoughts, and with the doctor on the stand, I had no sense of what Nick had experienced. Whitney Harris, Thelma Black, they'd made Nick seem real. The doctor was turning Nick into a case history.

I looked out the window. The lake was incredibly blue in the late morning sun. I studied the jurors. I jotted down that juror number eight was scratching his leg and that Dr. Dudley was saying Nick was running from the devil. I watched the doctor fish some more through his papers. He had put a manila folder on his lap. I watched

him reach into his pocket to take out a handkerchief and wipe the
perspiration from his face. I looked out of the window again. I
looked back at the doctor.

" 'I told him to move. I couldn't go around him. The contract
people were catching up to me. I got the gun and I shot it three
times.' " The doctor was reading the words Nick actually said
during the interview. " 'I was saying I was through, because something told me you've got to stop this sometime.' " They were powerful words. Nick must have trembled when he said them: Move. I'm
through. YOU'VE GOT TO STOP THIS SOMETIME! Powerful, but they didn't seem real because the doctor was mumbling.

The doctor said Nick told him he drove off after shooting the
man, then he drove back to see if anybody had been hurt, "which
reflected that there was something not quite logical about his thinking. Here earlier he'd shot him three times, and then he came back
to see if anyone was hurt. But then he continued with the hurt
theme," talking about how he'd been tormented at work, and prob-
lems he'd had paying his bills, and romantic frustrations, and how
he'd been victimized as a child. "He was mixed up as a child," the
doctor said. His father drank. Nick felt ashamed of that. Nick was
unable to relate to his father, "which points out that some authority
conflicts were going on in childhood."

"He's making it sound like Nick had trouble at work because he
couldn't get along with people in authority!" the reporter whispered
hoarsely.

"And like it was Nick's father who was reponsible for his illness,"
I added.

Dr. Dudley said he thought Nick never would have killed anyone
if it hadn't been for the fact that he was mentally ill. He said that on
October 21st Nick had been in such an acutely paranoid state he
couldn't have premeditated a murder or formulated an intent to kill
another human being. He said Nick was a schizophrenic, and he
gave a very long definition of schizophrenia, calling it a diseased state
of mind in which the individual has a derangement of thought pro-
cesses and dissociation of affect.

"Doctor, if Mr. Black had told you the following things: that he had
been having trouble at work, that he had been fired, that he had got
his job back, that he had lost his shop stewardship, that he was angry

over the treatment of blacks in America, that he was angry over International Machine Company's treatment of workers, that on the day in question when he came to work he was in a bad mood, that he left work, that he couldn't take the pressure, that he drove around, that he crashed into a car, that the guy wanted his license from him and, you know, in this mood he really couldn't be bothered giving him his license, he didn't want to go through the hassle of insurance company dealings, and all that, and the guy kept asking for his license, and he went back to his car and got a gun and walked back to the man and shot him in the head three times and left . . ."

The defender objected to the prosecutor's question which he said assumed facts not in evidence.

"I assume it's a hypothetical question?" the judge asked the prosecutor who was standing in front of Dr. Dudley.

"Yes," the prosecutor nodded.

"Objection overruled," the judge said. The law student whispered that hypothetical examples like that were allowed with expert witnesses.

"Even when they misstate the evidence?" I asked.

The student nodded. "The jurors will be told it's just a hypothetical example and not to treat it as evidence."

"Dr. Dudley, if you had been aware of the diagnosis by Dr. Ames a week after the incident that this defendant was faking psychosis, that there was nothing wrong with him, that he was faking because he had a heavy charge against him, would that have affected your opinion in any way, shape or form?" the prosecutor asked.

"Well, no, that wouldn't change my view if someone else came along and said it was a fake psychosis because I would question his competence," Dr. Dudley replied.

"You would question his competence? And if you had been aware that in light of Dr. Ames' opinion this defendant had been sent to the state mental hospital for further evaluation and that there had been an opinion by Dr. Claude Westover and Dr. Donna Rayburn, after interviews, after observations, for days and days, that it was fake psychosis, would that have affected your diagnosis, based on your one-hour interview?"

"If three people had said it was fake psychosis, I would go back and examine him again," the doctor replied, taking his handkerchief out of his pocket.

"Is it true that three people examined him for days and days and said he was faking?" I asked the reporter.

"I'm sure it isn't. I'm sure it's another hypothetical example," he answered.

"I wonder if the jury understands that," I said.

The prosecutor asked if Dr. Lamb, a psychiatrist scheduled to testify next for the defense, also said Nick was faking, would Dr. Dudley call him incompetent too. Wasn't it true that in insanity trials Dr. Dudley always testified for the defense? How could you possibly have an opinion about Nick's state of mind, Doctor, when you didn't examine him until two months after the shooting? Do you know anything about the coefficients of correlation? Are you familiar with the Rosenhahn study? Are you familiar with the draw-a-person test? Do you agree, Doctor, that any psychiatrist who wants to will find evidence of psychopathology in a patient? Is it correct that there are organic conditions which can cause behavior that is unwilled? Isn't what you call mental illness really a problem of psychological adjustment? Do you think it is a reasonable opinion that mental illness is a myth? Are you aware that hundreds of years ago, whenever a person did something out of the norm, the general populace ascribed that conduct to his body having been entered by demons and devils? Have you seen a demon, Doctor? Have you seen a mental illness? The prosecutor's words cracked like a whip.

"He's demolishing the doctor," the law student whispered.

"And Nick too," the reporter replied. "If Dr. Dudley looks bad, so does Nick."

I agreed.

Demons. Devils. The prosecutor was taking a whip after demons and devils. It wasn't Nick on trial. It was the field of psychiatry.

We took a break — Dr. Dudley had been testifying for hours — and when court reconvened the prosecutor had the doctor repeat what he'd told the defender: that Nick hadn't had the mental capacity to formulate an intent to kill. The doctor's statement was important, since it meant Nick couldn't be held legally responsible for murder, and the prosecutor went after it with another hypothetical example:

"Doctor, assume the following," the prosecutor said. "This defendant went to his car, and he got his gun, and then he shot the man three times, bang, bang, bang, in the head. Didn't he intend to kill him?"

"No," the doctor replied, explaining that the hypothetical example didn't say anything about motivation, what Nick was thinking at the time, who he thought the victim was. The doctor sounded reasonably sure of himself, but then the judge broke in.

"Assuming the facts of the hypothetical example to be true, did the defendant intend to kill the other person?" the judge asked.

"Well, your honor, it would seem that way."

"Doctor, assuming that the defendant is having his conversation with the man and going back to his car," the prosecutor took up the ball, "assuming he was getting the gun, putting the gun down by his side and shooting the man three times in the head — if those actions were in fact what happened, if those events and the conversation actually did take place, then at that time that person was manifesting an intention unlawfully to kill another human being, isn't that true?"

"Well, it's difficult for me to answer that," Dr. Dudley said. He was more forceful answering the prosecutor than he was answering the judge. "I would have to include some statements about his state of mind at the time, whether he thought this was a monster..."

The judge interrupted again. "Doctor, if I took this book and hit you over the head with it, would it be fair to say I intended to hit you?" He picked up a book from his desk. For a moment I expected him to use it.

"Yes..." the doctor replied. He started to say something more, but the judge was already onto the next question.

"So that if I took a gun and went bang, bang, you could draw certain conclusions from that?" he asked.

"Yes," Dr. Dudley murmured.

"So you could infer intent from an act as well as from what someone says?" the judge was glaring at the doctor.

"Well, I couldn't infer intent from an act in and of itself..."

"Boy, this judge and prosecutor are going out of their way to create confusion," the reporter whispered.

"The prosecutor is. His strategy is obviously to confuse the issue so that no matter what the doctor says, nobody will ever believe him," the law student replied.

"And the judge too," the reporter whispered.

"No, the judge is trying to get Dr. Dudley to speak to the law," the law student said. The trouble was that the law and psychiatry were talking about different things.

"If the law says you can tell what people intend to do by their actions, by their actions without knowing what's in their heads, then what's the point of a diminished capacity defense?" I whispered. "What's the point of all this psychiatric testimony?"

"You know, you two have been sitting all through the trial rooting for Nick," the student said. He sounded angry. "What happens if the jury *does* agree to manslaughter? In a few years Nick will be out. I sympathize with him, you know, I really do. It's pretty clear to me that he killed the guy because he was crazy. But what if he's let out in three or four years and has another spell and goes out and kills again?"

"That's the point," I agreed. It *was* the point, although I don't think I realized it until that minute. What becomes of Nick? How do we protect ourselves—and him? The evidence was overwhelming. Nick's friends, his family, his supervisor, the jailkeeper, everyone said something was terribly wrong with him, and the psychiatrist gave it a name. If that didn't constitute reasonable doubt about Nick's mental capacity, I didn't know what did. I'd asked the prosecutor earlier what it would have taken to win him over, and he'd replied that Nick would have had to have behaved oddly closer to the time of the shooting. It had seemed to me then that the prosecutor was placing the burden of proof on the defense when it was supposed to be the other way around. More than that, he was asking for absolute proof of Nick's diminished capacity.

"That's the point," I repeated. "How do we protect ourselves and Nick? But that's not what the jurors are being asked to consider. They aren't even permitted to ask the question. At the beginning of the trial, the judge actually told them not to think about punishment. He said that was the province of the courts and the social scientists.

"But what if Nick's behavior could be controlled by drugs? What if his family and friends could provide the supervision he needs? And if we don't know how to care for Nick without confining him, why do we have to confine him in prison as a criminal? Why must we hold him morally responsible for what he did? Those are the questions, but the alternatives before the jurors are prison or unsupervised freedom. The law is forcing them to turn Nick into a murderer."

The law student shrugged.

"No, really," I insisted. "The law has the defense use psychiatric testimony which ultimately hurts Nick. It asks a jury of strangers to read Nick's mind. It takes someone this scientific society should be perfectly able to see wasn't able to control his behavior, and it sets him up as a criminal."

The student, the reporter and I sat in silence. I guess we were all pretty upset. Dr. Dudley was looking for something in his manila folder, and I was acutely aware of the sounds of jurors coughing and the bailiff pushing back his chair.

The defense's second expert witness, Dr. Lamb, offered the same diagnosis as Dr. Dudley. He stood up better to the prosecutor and to the judge, so his presentation was more forceful, although he used a lot of technical words too and was difficult to understand.

Dr. Westover was the prosecutor's rebuttal witness. He was the white psychiatrist who'd examined Nick after the jail authorities had sent him to the state hospital. He said he'd first thought Nick was faking a psychosis to escape punishment, but because Nick's behavior was so bizarre, he'd had Dr. Rayburn, the psychologist, test him. When she decided that Nick *wasn't* faking, that he had something called Ganser syndrome, Dr. Westover said he changed his diagnosis to conform to hers. He told the prosecutor that Ganser syndrome is a psychosis people get from stress that impairs rationality, producing symptoms very similar to schizophrenia, with which it is often confused. He said he had no opinion about Nick's state of mind at the time of the shooting, that wasn't his job. Nick could have been psychotic when he shot the man, but he also could have been psychotic in the morning and then rational in the afternoon. The psychosis could have come and gone.

When the prosecutor delivered his closing argument to the jury, he called Nick a lousy worker. Nick stood up and seemed ready to lunge at him until the defender touched his arm and calmed him down.

The prosecutor told the jury he thought the psychiatric testimony had been utterly confusing. He said jurors had every right to rely on their own common sense instead. He said the defense psychiatrists had regurgitated legal phrases without understanding them. He said there were so many different diagnoses of Nick's condition, you could take your pick. He was as critical of his own psychiatric witness as he was of the defense's.

When the defender delivered his closing argument, he talked a lot about Whitney Harris and Frank Beecher and Thelma Black. He was eloquent, but I had trouble remembering the faces. Images of psychiatrists testifying and Nick lunging at the prosecutor crowded my mind.

THE VERDICT

The jury had been deliberating for several hours when the buzzer near the bailiff's desk sounded and he hurried out the side door and up the narrow stairs. He returned in a minute with a note from the foreman to the judge asking for the legal definition of murder and manslaughter in writing:

Judge,

The jury requests in writing the definitions of:

1) Premeditation and deliberation
2) Malice aforethought
   a) Implied
   b) Expressed
3) Diminished capacity

The judge had the bailiff call the jury down, and when the jurors and the lawyers and Nick were all assembled, the judge said, "Ladies and gentlemen, in terms of requesting in writing, the law hasn't gone that far at this point, so I will try and read these legal definitions slowly and clearly. If I am going too fast raise your hand . . ."

The next morning the bailiff's buzzer went off again, and the bailiff ran upstairs, returning with another note to the judge from the foreman:

Judge,

A juror brought in 12 copies of these definitions taken from Black's legal dictionary. Is it permissible to use them in our deliberations? Likewise, one juror extracted some definitions from a California law book ("a green book"). Should we use this information?

The judge sent the bailiff back with a negative reply.

At 3:40 that afternoon, after deliberating for a total of eight hours, the jury came down with a verdict:

> We the Jury in the above entitled case find the Defendant, Nicholas David Black, guilty of a felony, to wit, murder...

Two days later the second part of the trial began, the insanity phase which consisted of five more days of psychiatric testimony. The prosecutor had a new rebuttal witness, another white psychiatrist who said he'd examined Nick's record (he'd never examined Nick) and he'd found no basis for concluding that Nick was psychotic. During this phase of the trial the prosecutor was sharper and more caustic than he had been before. He called Nick a high school dropout who didn't believe he had to take responsibilty for his personal failures. He said Nick had been under the influence of radicals at work. He reminded the jury that Nick had once belonged to the Black Muslims who, he said, preached that white people were devils. He alluded to a trial in San Francisco of four Black Muslims accused of murdering whites as an initiation rite into their sect. He seemed to blame Nick for all that evil. It was as though the verdict in part one of the trial had released him from some constraint. It was as though there were then a tangible bond between him and the jury, and when the jury returned with the verdict that Nicholas Black was sane, it was as though the prosecutor and jurors were linked together, and together they'd given Nick a face.

Epilogue

Once I interviewed a prosecutor who told me he was convinced that the courts were a deterrent to crime, but not in the way most people thought. He said punishing robbers and burglars rarely reformed them, and it rarely deterred the kinds of people you'd expect to commit street crime. What it did was to set an example for middle class people. It kept middle class people in line, for they would rob and murder too if it weren't for fear of being labeled common criminals and losing social standing.

I was jolted by that, and I told the prosecutor he seemed very cynical to me. Not only was he accusing us all of being criminals at heart, but he was implying that our society needed criminals to control crime! We both laughed and we strayed to another subject, and I didn't think about the conversation again until after Nick's trial when the prosecutor's words suddenly seemed terribly important. If what he said was true, then street crime wasn't an accident or an anomaly. It was an institution rendering an important service. And criminals weren't accidents either. They were people who'd been nourished by poverty and racism, who'd been steered into careers in crime, who'd been raised to serve their country as keepers of law and order and to take the blame for everyone else's murderous passions. They were people who'd been raised to be scapegoats.

At Nick Black's trial I had the sense of watching a criminal in the making. I had a similar feeling when I watched Willie Monroe plead guilty; when I saw him go to prison for venting his anger by crashing into someone's car; when I saw Calvin Thompson charged as a felon for showing his resentment against the police. (If those two young men had been rich, society would have found some other way to deal with their anger.)

In Frazer's *Golden Bough* there's a glorious and detailed account of ancient scapegoating rituals where people tried to rid themselves of their misfortunes by transferring them to other beings and then casting those beings from their midst. There's a description of a sick man spilling his blood onto a goat so that others can lead the goat, and the sickness, far from the village. There's a description of returning warriors casting a woman slave out of their village in an effort to rid themselves of the smell of death. Villagers often killed their victims, combining the scapegoating with a sacrifice, cleansing their souls and fortifying their bodies with blood. They often chose as victims sickly people, people already doomed to die. Or they salved their consciences by choosing criminals. In transferring evil from themselves to others, they found relief. They tasted power.

Mrs. Drummond refused to reconsider her testimony against Willie Monroe. She *needed* him to be a criminal. She needed him as a scapegoat to carry away her fear. Tom White's grandmother refused to believe Nick Black was crazy. If she'd believed he was crazy, she'd have felt sympathy, when what she needed was someone to hate. She needed a murderer to send off to prison, carrying her grief with him.

Willie Monroe's prosecutor paraded before the jury with the gun, invoking images of young men hanging around liquor stores and plotting crimes, until all that was left of Willie Monroe's face was a scar. John Ramsey's and Marvin Washington's prosecutor paraded before the jury with a bloody pinstripe suit, passing out photos of bloody carpets and bloody clothing, until all that was left of John Ramsey was his incredible size, and all that was left of Marvin Washington was vicious eyes. Nick Black's prosecutor paraded in front of the jury too — with frightening images of communists and Black Muslims. Those defendants weren't tried as human beings. They were tried as devils. Their trials were contests between good and evil, quests for power.

After Nick Black's trial was over, the law student told me he thought I didn't have enough concern for the victims of street crime. I told him that wasn't true. But I didn't believe that filling up prisons would offer the relief he was seeking. There would always be criminals loose on the streets because the society was too dependent on crime. There were too many people whose jobs depended on crime: Policemen who patrolled the ghettos and barrios, security guards who patrolled the supermarkets, burglar alarm salesmen who peddled their wares, judges and lawyers who staffed the courts, wardens and guards who staffed the prisons. There were too many business and political leaders who depended on crime too—people of wealth and power who cried about crime in the streets to divert attention from their own stupidity and greed as they climbed to heights on the backs of criminals.

I asked him how much was resolved by holding Lorenzo Smith or Franklin Butler responsible for their crimes when their criminality was of society's making. How much was resolved by holding them responsible when they were so lacking in power? In relying on punishment to solve the problem we obscured the causes and perpetuated crime. We set powerless people against one another, sapping their energy, killing their dreams of a humane society where there wouldn't be such powerlessness and fear, or the need for crime.

About the Author

During the 1960's, Harriet Ziskin worked in Washington D.C. as an education specialist for the House Education and Labor Committee, a civil rights compliance officer for the U.S. Office of Education, and a research specialist for the U.S. Commission on Civil Rights. In 1968, she moved to the San Francisco Bay Area where she became involved in grassroots politics. Her doctoral dissertation was a study of how the development of the school system bureaucracy diminished democratic control in Oakland. As a freelance reporter she has written investigative reports and political analyses for numerous local newspapers. She has covered the Oakland school system, Oakland city government, and the Alameda County courts. She also writes fiction.

About the Artist

A native of Panama City, Florida, Jimi Evins graduated with distinction in painting from the California College of Arts and Crafts where he studied with Vincent Perez. He has also studied in Vancouver, Canada; Kingston, Jamaica; and Ile-Ife, Nigeria. His work has been exhibited widely in the San Francisco Bay Area, and he has had exhibits in Florida and Nigeria.

The Contemporary Literature Series

An alternative publishing project featuring quality literature concerning important social issues. Also in the series are:

Letters to Nanette by Bob Biderman. This novel is about a young man who ended up in the peacetime army a year before the Vietnam War became real. His is an allegorical, absurd adventure that leads from the cafes of Berkeley to an army training unit in Georgia where reluctant draftees are taught the elements of jungle warfare. Written with warmth, humor and understanding, it is a story of a special kind of courage and honor.

Green Leaves Turn Red by Joy Magezis. A novel about a young woman growing up in the turmoil of the '60's who evolves from a naive, working-class girl into a questioning New Left organizer. It is a sensitive and fast-paced account about the people and forces involved in the political activity of the time that lays the groundwork for understanding the rebirth of the feminist movement and the development of the turbulent student movement of the late '60's. *Scheduled for publication in 1983.*

Early Stages Press
PO Box 31463, San Francisco CA 94131

Please send me ____ copies of *The Blind Eagle* @ $6.95 (paper); $12.95 (hard)

____ copies of *Letters to Nanette* @ $5.95 (paper); $11.95 (hard)

(Add $1 for postage and handling; in California add 6% tax.)

Enclosed is $ _____

Name _____

Address _____

_____ Zip _____